Summer Paradis and Sandra Vivian Graul

NOTORIOUS
NEW ENGLAND

A TRAVEL GUIDE TO TRAGEDY AND TREACHERY

Schiffer Publishing Ltd

4880 Lower Valley Road · Atglen, PA 19310

Other Schiffer Books by the Author:

Gone But Not Forgotten: New England's Ghost Towns, Cemeteries, & Memorials (with Cathy McManus) ISBN: 978-0-7643-4552-4

New England's Scariest Stories and Urban Legends (with Cathy McManus) ISBN: 978-0-7643-4122-9

Other Schiffer Books on Related Subjects:

More New England Graveside Tales. T. M. Gray
ISBN: 978-0-7643-3585-3

More Lost Loot: Ghostly New England Treasure Tales. Patricia Hughes
ISBN: 978-0-7643-3627-0

"Schiffer," "Schiffer Publishing, Ltd.," and the pen and inkwell logo are registered trademarks of Schiffer Publishing, Ltd.

Cover design by Matt Goodman
Designed by Brenda McCallum

Type set in Tungsten/Zurich/Times New Roman
ISBN: 978-0-7643-5571-4
Printed in China

Published by Schiffer Publishing, Ltd.
4880 Lower Valley Road
Atglen, PA 19310
Phone: (610) 593-1777; Fax: (610) 593-2002
E-mail: Info@schifferbooks.com
Web: www.schifferbooks.com

For our complete selection of fine books on this and related subjects, please visit our website at www.schifferbooks.com. You may also write for a free catalog.

Schiffer Publishing's titles are available at special discounts for bulk purchases for sales promotions or premiums. Special editions, including personalized covers, corporate imprints, and excerpts, can be created in large quantities for special needs. For more information, contact the publisher.

We are always looking for people to write books on new and related subjects. If you have an idea for a book, please contact us at proposals@schifferbooks.com.

TO OUR JUNIOR PARANORMAL INVESTIGATORS IN TRAINING
(JACOB PARSONS AND CHASE DOUCETTE) AND OUR FELLOW TAPHOPHILES EVERYWHERE.

ACKNOWLEDGMENTS

This book would not have been possible without the support of all our family and friends and those who encouraged and helped us along the way. A special thank you to our wonderful editor, Dinah Roseberry, and the rest of the gang at Schiffer Publishing.

SUMMER:
For my one true love, my amazing son, Jacob Parsons. You are my everything. Also a huge "Thank You" to my parents, Bob and Karin Langdon Paradis, for understanding why writing is so important to me and removing any and all obstacles to make this book come together. I hope I've made you proud.

SANDRA:
I want to acknowledge foremost my children—Kaylee, Jayna, and Chase—for being the beautiful, patient, and inquisitive beings they are, and for allowing me time to work on this project. I love you with all my heart and soul. I also want to thank my family and close friends who have indulged and supported me in this endeavor, which seemed to have no end! I also give thanks to my friend and coauthor, Summer, who invited me to step into this adventure and fully experience what book writing is all about!

In hopes that this book encourages anyone who reads it to really see and feel the world around them, no matter how close or how far they may venture, we leave you with this thought:

NOT ALL ARE LOST FOR THE WANDERING,
FOR THERE IS MUCH BEAUTY AND KNOWLEDGE
TO BE DISCOVERED IN THE JOURNEY.

Contents

Introduction

DARK TOURISM

Noun—Dark tourism is the act of travel and visitation to sites, attractions, and exhibitions that have real or re-created death, suffering, or the seemingly macabre as a main theme.

Around the world, there are many who seek out these less conventional travel destinations, and visitors to such sites—such as Auschwitz, Ground Zero, Gettysburg battlefields, and Alcatraz Prison—have skyrocketed. In the following pages you will find an unconventional and eclectic travel guide to New England's darker histories and tales. Everyone from history aficionados to paranormal enthusiasts will find topics to engage them, from serial killers to infamous haunted locales to historic homes and cemeteries.

Presented from west to east across northern and then southern New England, each section is arranged by state in a roughly northern to southern flow. Featuring a balance of old favorites and new finds, we endeavored to present you with just enough information to whet your appetite and show why the site is notable to New England history. We have included helpful tips for how to find the locations, both geographically and logistically, with on-site landmarks and the best time to plan your travel. Care was taken to consider the diverse needs of visitors, noting when age ranges or mobility may be factors, as well as the always important where to park, where to eat, and where to find a clean restroom!

We hope the many stories and photographs will inspire you to plan your own adventures to New England's most notorious destinations.

Emily's Bridge

STOWE, VERMONT

SITE HISTORY

New England is known for its beautiful covered bridges, and the Gold Brook Bridge, built in 1844 in lovely Stowe, Vermont, is one of the most renowned around. The bridge on Covered Bridge Road is a popular place by day for photographing and sightseeing, but by night the bridge draws a different type of tourist—thrill seekers looking for its resident ghost, Emily.

Emily's story and how she came to haunt the bridge is a sad tale. She was one of the most lovely and desirable young women in Stowe, and there was no shortage of young men who desired her. Though many approached her parents to express their interest in her, they were exceptionally strict and felt that no men in town were worthy of their darling daughter, so she was left with no suitors.

Her parent's disapproval was enough to keep many away until one special young man felt Emily's love would be worth chancing her parents' wrath. He and Emily had been sneaking away to be together, away from her parents' watchful eyes. Months passed and the couple desired to be married. Emily eagerly accepted his proposal, and he excitedly went to ask for her parents' blessings, sure that they would be moved by Emily's happiness. He thought wrong.

Emily's parents forcibly removed her suitor from their home and forbade her from seeing him again. Not to be swayed so easily, they planned to meet at the Gold Brook Bridge to elope and begin a life together. Sadly, her parents caught wind of their plan and hired thugs to beat him and prevent him from making the rendezvous, thinking Emily would soon return home. Emily arrived at the bridge with her belongings and waited for her love. As dawn approached, she feared that he had gotten cold feet and couldn't

Emily's Bridge in Stowe, Vermont.

bear the thought of returning home to her controlling parents. Using a rope that had bundled her luggage together, she climbed to the rafters of the bridge, where she hanged herself in the place where she had hoped to start her new life.

Despite the horrific beating, Emily's love continued his way to the bridge. Due to the nature of his injuries, it took him the entire night to arrive, where he tragically found Emily's lifeless body. He collapsed at the site—whether from his injuries or a broken heart is debatable—and *he* passed away as well. Though his name has been lost to history, Emily's has not, and her spirit is said to remain on the spot—and she is not happy.

Over the years, the bridge has earned a fierce reputation as one of Vermont's most haunted locations. Walkers have reported being scratched, hearing a woman's cries for help, hearing the creaking noise of a heavy weight hanging from a rope, seeing a white mist, and seeing Emily's full-bodied apparition. Emily seems to have a particular dislike for automobiles, and there have been frequent tales of scratched paint jobs and stalled car engines.

AUTHOR'S NOTE

I visited Emily's Bridge while researching topics for *New England's Scariest Stories and Urban Legends* with coauthor Cathy McManus. We took some lovely pictures during the day and eagerly anticipated our evening investigation. When we returned at night, we found several other groups there, including tourists and fellow paranormal investigators. We ran audio that appeared to indicate some electronic voice phenomena (EVPs), but due to the constant river noise, we didn't consider this evidence conclusive. When we attempted to take photographs of the bridge, we experienced some significant camera malfunctions, and even when using many different cameras, flashes, and tripods, we were not able to take clear pictures, each picture appearing fuzzy.

With hopes of gathering photographic evidence dashed and having experienced a notable cold spot nearby, we tried our hand at a Ghost Box session, using a handheld radio that had been modified to continuously scan the radio dials without stopping, which the spirits can use to communicate with investigators in real time.

The distinct messages received, however, were that we were not welcome at the bridge. We all heard quite clearly the phrases "Go away," "Dead," "Go," and "Bye." We decided to visit her grave the following morning and wished Emily well and hoped that she would someday find peace. —S. P.

The interior of Emily's Bridge.

DIRECTIONS

Emily's Bridge is located on Covered Bridge Road in Stowe, Vermont. Her grave, labeled Emiline, is located at the Old Yard Cemetery at 51 Main Street.

ALSO NEARBY

The final resting places of the Trapp family, whose story was famously, if loosely, told in *The Sound of Music,* are located beside the Trapp Family Lodge, located at 700 Trapp Hill Road in Stowe.

Joseph Smith LDS Memorial

SOUTH ROYALTON, VERMONT

SITE HISTORY

If I had revealed all that has been made known
to me, scarcely a man on this stand would stay with me.
And Brother, if I were to tell you all I know of
the Kingdom of God, I do know that you will rise
up and kill me.

—Joseph Smith Jr.

Joseph Smith Jr. was an American religious leader regarded as a "Prophet of God," and he was the first president and founder of Mormonism and the Latter Day Saints movement. Born on the Sharon and South Royalton, Vermont, town lines, Smith rose to prominence and published the Book of Mormon at the age of twenty-four. Fourteen years later, he had amassed tens of thousands of followers, had established a settlement, was named mayor of Nauvoo, Illinois, and was rumored to be planning a campaign for president of the United States.

Despite amassing popularity among his followers, he had also earned heavy criticism from non-Mormons; in particular, for his support of plural marriage. By some reports, Smith himself had as many as thirty wives. When several seceders from the church formed a newspaper called the *Nauvoo Expositor*, they released their one and only issue exposing Smith's polygamous ways, much to his ire. He declared that the paper was "a public nuisance" and

ordered the town marshal to destroy their facilities, which he did on June 10, 1844. The general public decried the violation of the freedom of the press, and Smith reacted by declaring martial law on June 18, 1844.

The state government charged Smith with inciting a riot and treason against the state of Illinois, and Joseph and his brother, Hyrum, surrendered to the police to await trial. The Smiths never had their day in court, since on June 27, 1844, a mob of 200 men—faces painted black with wet gunpowder—forced their way into the jailhouse and shot and killed both men where they sat in their cell. The crime earned both men instant martyrdom within the Mormon community.

Dedicated in 1905, on the one hundredth anniversary of Joseph Smith's birth, the centerpiece of the memorial site is the ninety-nine-ton granite obelisk that is reportedly the "World's Largest Polished Shaft." Though the height of the entire monument measures fifty-two feet, the obelisk itself measures exactly thirty-eight and one-half feet, one foot for each year Smith was alive. Buried beneath the monument is a time capsule containing documents important to the Latter-Day Saints (LDS) community. The monument is at the top of a small hill surrounded by 350 acres of landscaped grounds and wooded homestead site areas. Speakers around the site play music performed by the Mormon Tabernacle Choir. Displays about the life of Joseph Smith Jr., including the hearthstone from the Solomon Mack farm where Smith was born and lived for the first three years of his life, are on display in the visitor center on the site.

The sign at Prophet Joseph Smith's birthplace.

DIRECTIONS

The Joseph Smith Jr. Birthplace Memorial is located at 357 LDS Lane, off Dairy Hill Road in South Royalton, Vermont. The site is handicapped accessible, with free parking and admission year-round. The monument and homestead foundations are viewable at any time, but the visitor center and guided tours are available November through April,

Monday–Saturday from 9:00 a.m.–5:00 p.m., Sunday 1:30–5:00 p.m.; May through October, Monday–Saturday from 9:00a.m.–7:00 p.m., Sunday 1:30–7:00 p.m.; and December daily from 9:00 a.m. to 9:00 p.m., with holiday light displays that are regarded as some of the best in the state.

More information about visiting the historic site is available at www.lds.org/locations/joseph-smith-birthplace-memorial?lang= eng&_r=1#d.

VERMONT

Wilson Castle

PROCTOR, VERMONT

SITE HISTORY

There is a magnificent work of architectural craftsmanship just outside the Green Mountain National Forest called Wilson Castle. This fabulous piece of art, which was initially used as a family home, was built in 1867 by Vermont native Dr. John Johnson and was commissioned by his wife, Lady Johnson, a member of an aristocratic English family. The story goes, as told by the current owner and curator Ms. Denise Davine, that Dr. Johnson traveled to England to pursue his medical studies, where he met a young lady from a wealthy family. They married and set upon the adventure of building a family estate in Dr. Johnson's home state of Vermont.

The castle grounds were made up of the main house and eighteen outbuildings across 115 acres of land and had a final cost of $1.3 million (approximately twenty million dollars adjusted for today's inflation). The castle boasts over thirty rooms spread over three floors, a beautiful array of eighty-four stained-glass windows, and thirteen oversized and ornate fireplaces. The castle's early history is sad in that the Johnsons had resided at the completed castle for only a short time before Lady Johnson passed away; following her death, Dr. Johnson could not keep up with the high costs of maintenance to the property, and it fell into a bad way, becoming known to locals as "Johnson's Folly."

After the death of Dr. Johnson, the castle changed hands quite a few times until 1939, when Army Signal Corps engineer Colonel Herbert Wilson (known around the castle as "The Colonel"), who

Wilson Castle in Proctor, Vermont.

was looking for a family summer home, bought it for the back-taxes sum of $12,000 from the town of Proctor, as his granddaughter, Denise, explained during our visit. The Colonel bought it "as is" with much of the contents from the English originators still in place. The Colonel was a gifted engineer and pioneer in the AM radio field and installed a radio tower and station on the estate grounds. The Colonel permanently retired to the castle in the 1950s and began extensive work on the home, which included art and architectural installations by well-celebrated European artisans as well as making important functional improvements to the castle.

The home was fully operational, lived in, and even opened for tours in the 1960s. The castle is filled with fabulous relics, antiques, books, works of art, and mementos from around the world. Over the years, the Colonel added to the collection while being stationed in England, Bali, and Indonesia. He had requested particular items as payment in lieu of cash for radio and communications work done overseas, and he had them shipped back to Vermont to furnish the home. The Colonel also commissioned original design trade work done by some well-known European craftsmen and artisans, such as for elaborate tile and wood floors, fireplace mantles and encasements, door frame woodwork, ceiling paintings, and colorful stained-glass window treatments.

Due to some documented and shared unexplained and mysterious experiences by visitors, as well as eyewitness reports by the caretakers and residents of the castle, it is often included in listings of haunted places in Vermont. The sounds of a woman crying in Lady Johnson's bedroom, strange mists and orbs appearing in photographs, phantom footsteps, and glimpses of full-bodied apparitions all have been reported. Spirits from the past are heard playing billiards on the second floor, and the organ and music boxes on the first floor sound without human interaction. The castle itself is believed to be very much alive with the presence of those who have lived and worked on the grounds.

Top: Wilson Castle veranda. Bottom: Lady Johnson's bedroom.

AUTHOR'S NOTE

In our opinion, the castle is haunted by one or more of the past residents, as we experienced firsthand during our visit. We did get the distinct feeling, as soon as we began walking up the rocky dirt drive to the front of the castle grounds, that someone, specifically female, watches from the upper left window. As we were touring the rooms we discovered that this was the main bedroom of the lady of the home (Lady Johnson, later followed by Mrs. Wilson) and what is now called the Wedding or Bridal Suite.

Upon entering the castle, I felt a very comfortable, calm, peaceful, and strangely familiar feeling. This place immediately felt like "home" to me, and I just wanted to stay there all day and all night! I did feel a presence from time to time in the lady's bedroom, and we did distinctly hear a faint "Yes" reply to a question that we had asked each other out loud, about the possible mindset of the spirit that may be present

Family member and owner Denise Davine has strived and struggled to keep the castle in her family. Current and continued plans are to create fundraising events not only to showcase the home but to bring together those who are interested, either from a historical or otherworldly view. She is working on major restoration projects in all phases of the building's rehabilitation, as well as toward reinstating the building's historical certificate in the state of Vermont. During our interview and castle tour, Ms. Davine shared strange experiences that she believes were visits or communications from her deceased mom or grandmother, and also possibly Lady Johnson, while in the castle.

Some believe that the original matron of the house, Lady Johnson, haunts it because she is sad. Others believe that the current owner's mother or grandmother is present in the home. My feeling is that this place is not a place of haunting, horrible tragedies, or even strange events, but rather where spirits linger as a lasting tribute to a beloved home, and that is an imprinted feeling that sticks with you for centuries.

Denise's grandniece, Armani, was a very cute and intelligent ten-year-old who takes an interest in conservation of her ancestral home and the ghostly goings on within. Her grandaunt greatly hopes that she will be the next caretaker of the castle, and we wholeheartedly agree. We had a beautiful visit, although much too short for our liking, and we would love the opportunity to return!
—S. G.

DIRECTIONS

Wilson Castle is located at 2970 West Proctor Road in Proctor, Vermont. The castle itself is set back off the road but does have a modest sign at the entrance of the driveway. If you've passed it (like we did!) you may notice the veranda side of the castle sitting high up on the hill on a second pass down the road. The estate also sprawls across the street, where you will also notice the animal barns, brick carriage houses, and tall radio antenna. More information about visiting the property can be accessed at www.wilsoncastle.com.

Grave of President Calvin Coolidge

PLYMOUTH, VERMONT

SITE HISTORY

Calvin Coolidge served as the twenty-ninth vice president of the United States, during Warren G. Harding's controversial presidency. The Vermont-born lawyer, who had risen to political prominence in Massachusetts, eventually serving as governor, earned praise for being a decisive leader for his handling of the 1919 Boston police strike. A man of quiet and steadfast nature, he earned the nickname of "Silent Cal" and avoided many of the stigmas affixed to President Harding after his participation in the Teapot Dome bribery scandal, the discovery of multiple extramarital affairs, and an illegitimate daughter conceived during his time in office.

While on his Voyage of Understanding tour of the United States, President Harding suffered a fatal heart attack at San Francisco's Palace Hotel on August 2, 1923. Coolidge was at his family home in Plymouth, Vermont, when he was informed of the death, and that very evening he was quickly and quietly sworn into office in his family living room, using his family Bible. He earned the notable distinction of being the only US president to be sworn into office by a parent; his father, a local justice of the peace, was granted the honor of conducting the ceremony.

The final resting place of President Calvin Coolidge.

Coolidge served as the thirtieth president of the United States from 1923 to 1929, encompassing much of the Roaring Twenties. He earned a favorable approval rating and was easily elected in his own right in the 1924 election. He holds the distinction of being the first president to make a public radio address to the American public and is the only president ever to have been born on the 4th of July.

He died suddenly of coronary thrombosis four years after leaving office at "The Beeches," his home in North Hampton, Massachusetts, which he had built with his wife, Grace. Coolidge is buried at Plymouth Notch Cemetery in Plymouth, Vermont, the largest and only still-operational cemetery in the town; his simple stone bears the Great Seal of the United States. His tombstone is commensurate in size and grandeur with the majority of the markers surrounding it and speaks to his conservative frugality that he was remembered for.

Coolidge family plot.

DIRECTIONS

Plymouth Notch Cemetery is located on Lynds Hill Road in Plymouth, Vermont. The cemetery is arranged neatly on a steep hill just down the road from Coolidge's childhood home. Though there is no designated parking for the cemetery, there is ample room to pull safely over along the stone wall beside the front of the cemetery. Visitors enter the cemetery by climbing a series of stone steps, and the Coolidge family plot is just to the left of the stairs on the second level. Though the plot may cause difficulties to approach for those with mobility issues, its proximity to the street makes it easily viewable from outside the rock wall. The cemetery is open year-round, daily from dawn to dusk.

ALSO NEARBY

The President Calvin Coolidge State Historic Sites are located at 3780 Route 100A in Plymouth, Vermont. Open daily May through October and weekdays from November through April, you can visit the General Store apartment where Coolidge was born, the family homestead where he was sworn into office, the church's presidential pew from which the family worshiped, and the space Coolidge staffers used as an alternate Oval Office during the summer months.

Bowman Mausoleum

CUTTINGSVILLE, VERMONT

SITE HISTORY

John Porter Bowman was born in 1816, in Pierce's Corner, Clarendon, Vermont. The son of a farmer, he chose a different path and moved to Rutland, Vermont, to learn the tanning trade. There he learned the skills that led him to begin to find success in general tanning and currying boots and shoes. In 1849, he married Jennie E. Gates, and they began to create a life together in Stony Creek, New York, where he made a small fortune selling leather goods to the US Government during the Civil War.

Family success was not as achievable as his business success, however. A daughter, Addie, was born in 1854 but died at the age of four months. A second daughter, Ella, came along in 1860, and though she lived to the age of nineteen, a sudden illness also took her to an untimely early grave. The Bowmans were devastated, and John's grief was amplified when Jennie passed away the following year, in 1879.

Consumed by grief, John became determined to build them a final resting place worthy of their memories. After failing to find a suitable location in New York or his hometown in Vermont, Bowman discovered a small burying yard in Cuttingsville, Vermont, that would be suitable, and he purchased all the adjoining land, hiring New York architect and mortuary artist G. B. Croff to design a shrine.

For over a year, 125 skilled sculptors, granite and marble cutters, masons, and laborers erected the only mausoleum in the newly renamed Laurel Glen Cemetery. The rectangular pediment-front mausoleum was constructed from 750 tons of granite, 50 tons of marble, 20,000 bricks, 525 barrels of English portland cement, 10 barrels of calcined plaster, and 100 loads of sand. Designed with classical and Egyptian elements with an exceptionally extravagant interior, which was unlike most structures of its kind, and it was clearly meant to be seen.

The statue of John P. Bowman in front of the Bowman Mausoleum.

The walls and ceilings were lined in Brocadilla marble, with English encaustic tile flooring, marble carved into wainscoting, and panels and columns having large mirrors placed to give the appearance of a larger space. Busts bearing the resemblances of Jennie and Ella and a statue of baby Addie all are displayed in front of the vertically stacked family tombs, underneath a lintel engraved with the dedication, "Sacred to the memory of a sainted wife and daughters." Above the vault is inscribed "a couch of dreamless sleep" and "rest" surrounded with laurel branches below. A frieze with a floral pattern circles the interior and sides of the vault.

In 1880 the mausoleum was completed, and in 1881 the women's caskets were reinterred in the mausoleum. John made significant improvements to the cemetery, with the grounds being graded, two fountains being installed, a retaining wall with three gates being constructed, and additional grassy lots and seating areas and walkways of crushed purple slate being laid.

With the mausoleum and cemetery improvements completed, Bowman commissioned Croff to begin to construct a mansion to be used as a summer residence directly across the street from the cemetery, naming it Laurel Hall. He further ordered the building of a greenhouse, conservatory, icehouse, carriage barn, and care-taker's cottage, creating what he named Laurel Glen. The mausoleum and grounds became a popular tourist attraction, with many people traveling from considerable distances by carriage to the elaborate tomb and to picnic on the grounds. The site became so popular that according to the *Rutland Daily Herald* and *Globe*, it reportedly received 10,000 visitors during the 1881 season alone, and Bowman had to hire an usher to give brief guided tours and add a wooden stand to hold a guest book outside the mausoleum.

A life-size statue of Mr. Bowman, still very much alive at the time, was posed at the top of the stairs outside the mausoleum. Bent over in grief and wrapped in his mourning cloak, silk hat, and gloves, he carries a funeral wreath and a key in his hand. He returned to Laurel Hall in 1887 and looked out at his own image and the remains of his loved ones until he passed away on the property in 1891.

As with any old property near a cemetery, Laurel Hall earned its share of postmortem rumors. In his will, in addition to funds being left to maintain the mausoleum in perpetuity, were stipulations that listed that the house and grounds were to be left exactly as they were at the time of Bowman's death. Stories circulated in the Cuttingsville community that Bowman believed in reincarnation and that his servants were ordered to prepare dinner nightly in case Bowman and his family returned. Later, ghost stories and tales of hidden money surfaced, and a future tenant of Laurel Hall ran a small business named "The Haunted Mansion Book Shop" on the property.

AUTHOR'S NOTE

Opening and closing of the seasonal coverings varies, so you may wish to check with the Shrewsbury Historical Society, which currently maintains the property (phone— 802-492-3324; website— www.shrewsburyhistoricalsociety.com). We made the mistake of traveling from Maine to Vermont over a Memorial Day weekend to be greatly disappointed that the mausoleum had not been unveiled for the year. Though we were glad that we chose to make a return visit, we do highly recommend that you make a quick check with the Shrewsbury Historical Society prior to planning your trip to view this hauntingly beautiful piece of mortuary arts.—S. P.

DIRECTIONS

Laurel Glen cemetery is located on Route 103 in Cuttingsville, Vermont. Parking can be achieved by pulling safely over along the edge of Route 103 and entering the cemetery grounds by foot. Please note that the statue of Mr. Bowman is covered by a metal enclosure during the winter months, and a winter door covers the summer gate to protect the stonework

Phineas Gage Memorial

CAVENDISH, VERMONT

SITE HISTORY

Many New Englanders may be unfamiliar with the tragic story of what happened to a gentleman named Phineas Gage in Cavendish, Vermont. The railroad foreman, who worked in Vermont but originally came from neighboring New Hampshire, continues to be quite an infamous medical anomaly resulting from a freak accident, which is still studied by neuroscientists to this day. His case is widely known as the landmark "American Crowbar Case."

On the afternoon of September 13, 1848, Phineas Gage, then approximately twenty-five years of age, was directing a construction crew preparing a railway bed for the Rutland & Burlington Railroad by blasting rock in the growing industrial area of Cavendish. The account goes that Mr. Gage was holding a tamping iron that was resting inside a blasting hole. He had just turned his head back to his crew in order to speak to them, a move that inadvertently aligned his head with the actual blasting hole. What happened next, I am sure, was the ultimate nightmare of all mothers and spouses of railroad workers. It seemed that a spark from movement of the tamping iron inside the hole set off the blast, prematurely sending the iron with piercing speed up out of the ground and straight through Phineas's head. The three-foot-seven-inch-long, one-and-a-quarter-inch-diameter, thirteen-and-a-half-pound iron rod quite literally rocketed through Phineas's skull. It pierced the left side of his head, entering at the jaw just under the cheekbone, passed behind the eye socket, cutting through the brain, and exited on the right frontal side of his skull. When the rod was

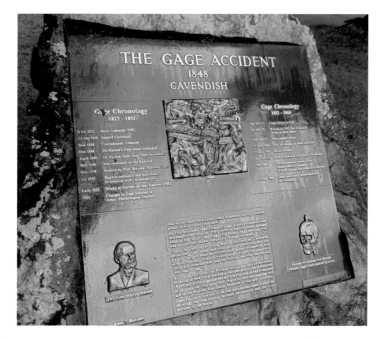

Phineas Gage memorial.

found a short distance away, witnesses reported seeing brain matter and blood on it.

Unbelievably, Mr. Gage survived this grotesque and deadly injury. In fact, after having displayed a bout of seizure-like activity then referred to as "convulsions," accounts have it that Phineas actually spoke a few minutes later. He then walked with little assistance to a waiting wooden cart and sat upright on the ride into town to the hotel where he was staying, so they could request help. His medical status immediately following this event, in this time period before modern medicine and understanding of neuroscience,

VERMONT

to say the least was an amazing example of scientific curiosity and human survival.

Dr. Edward H. Williams was the treating physician on site and had commented that he thought the story of Mr. Gage's injury being from a tamping rod that sliced through his head was not true and was a possible exaggeration. He soon realized—after seeing a blood-covered Phineas bend over and throw up, causing him to lose about "half a teacup" (approximate measuring comparisons in those days) of brain matter, which fell onto the floor from the funnel-shaped hole in his head—that it was all too horrendously true!

The discussion regarding how "lucky" or "unlucky'" Phineas was that fateful day goes on to this day. His case has been studied by physicians and neuroscientists far and wide and was profiled by the likes of the *Harvard Gazette*, the *Smithsonian*, and the *American Phrenology Journal* (a theoretic study of the skull that is now defunct).

A strange though fortunate factor was how the tamping rod used by Phineas sailed so sharply and so smoothly through his head. This was because it was made a bit differently than typical rods of the time. The point was tapered and the whole rod was fairly smooth, as well—it did not have the bent claw at the end (hence the name "crowbar") that the usual rods would have. Apparently, the owner of this rod commissioned it to be made this way. Phineas did lose the sight and function of his left eye as the rod severed the optic nerves, but the path of the rod missed certain other critical points that facilitated his survival.

The actual brain damage was further studied as recently as 2012, when scientists reconstructed his skull and brain and followed the possible path of the rod. It was determined that the consequence that Phineas experienced following this injury was posttraumatic personality change due to the permanent interruption of the communication of the emotional limbic system to the frontal cortex. We now know that this results in erratic, unpredictable behavior, and that these patients can display uninhibited behavior that can seem uncontrolled. This contributed to persons who did not personally know Gage to deem him a social outcast, unable to control himself, rude, vulgar, animallike, and not able to work or support himself. It is agreed, however, that these descriptions of Gage were widely exaggerated, since there is more evidence, especially from his physicians and close friends and family, that he was a kind, levelheaded, astute, businesslike, and fair-minded man prior to his injury and had only sporadic episodes of this uncontrolled behavior. In fact, during his convalescence while being treated, Phineas was reported to have said there was no need for his railroad crew to visit him, since he would be back at his post in quick form. This proved his propensity to work. His recovery, of course, took much longer than he was hoping. He had drifted in and out of a comatose-like state for quite some time before he would be able to sit himself up in bed and then slowly get back to walking and such.

Scientifically and psychologically, he was celebrated as the first example of a person surviving a traumatic brain injury, and much was learned from him, but he did suffer for this "survival" the remainder of his life. Over the next eleven and a half years, he experienced epileptic seizures and most likely had terrible headaches comparable to what we now know as migraines. His progress in these years of his life captured a nation's interest. There were exaggerated stories of Gage joining P. T. Barnum's freak show circus, which were not true. He did attempt to support himself through self-promotion in his local area in New England and appearances at Barnum's American Museum in New York City, but this was not the traveling freak show that Barnum is now remembered for.

Phineas went on to do something quite amazing, which was thought to be driven by his need to work and his need to be somewhere that people didn't know him and, therefore, weren't able to judge him. He traveled to South America and worked as a long-distance stagecoach driver. This was an amazing feat that showed that he was able to control (most of the time) his psychological and emotional urges. It required a great deal of stamina, strength, patience, and interaction with people. As well, the stagecoach he drove was powered by six horses and was reported as a sight to be behold as one man commanded all six animals.

In the end, as he was feeling increasingly weak and experienced more headaches and seizures, Phineas returned home to his mother and other family members, who had now relocated to Santa Clara, California. With his anxiousness to keep working, he did a brief stint with a local farmer there, but fell increasingly ill. Phineas Gage died at his home in Santa Clara at the age of thirty-six on May 21, 1860. He was buried there and later exhumed at the request of his Harvard surgeon, Henry Jacob Bigelow, and with agreement of his family, who did want more information about his injury and the cause of his personality change. Phineas Gage's skull and the tamping rod that pierced it, as well as a "life mask" made while he was a patient of Dr. Bigelow's, all are on display at Harvard Medical School campus, as it has been since the 1860s.

More recently, the first daguerreotype photograph of Gage has been discovered, officially identified, and recorded into history. This image was discovered thanks to modern technology and a picture-posting site online. Jack and Beverly Wilgus, a couple from Massachusetts who loved to collect old antique photographs, acquired this particular one that they called "The Whaler" and held it in their collection for thirty years. They began posting their collection on Flickr.com and referred to the gentleman in the photo as a whaler. An anonymous but astute observer messaged them that this was not a whaling harpoon in the picture but could, incredibly, be the only known photo of Phineas Gage and the tamping rod that pierced through his head. Soon the Wilguses made a visit to the Warren Anatomical Museum at Harvard Medical School in Boston to investigate the possibility. Everything matched up—the facial points, the scar, and the inscription on the tamping rod. What an amazing find! The photo is now on display and completes Mr. Gage's exhibit at the museum.

AUTHOR'S NOTE

Driving through Cavendish (sister town to Proctorsville), where their motto is "Your Place in the Woods," is just what you would expect a small rural town near the Green Mountains of Vermont to look and feel like. It is located in a valley just over the New Hampshire border, surrounded by the lush summer greenery of the ski areas of the Okemo State Forest, Killington, Rutland, and Woodstock.

During the late 1700s through late 1800s, Cavendish was a booming industrial town full of mills and manufacturing businesses. Most of these businesses and buildings are long gone. The town was obviously very old looking but neat, tidy, and quiet the midsummer day when we visited. Although listed as a "notable person" on the modern Wikipedia website town profile, the official town website of Cavendish does not list the Phineas Gage event within their initial "History Thumbnail" page. Mr. Gage's event is listed in the Cavendish Historical Society News web page outlining a walking tour of the connected villages of Cavendish and Proctorsville that you could embark upon at your own leisure. —S. G.

DIRECTIONS

Cavendish, Vermont, is located not far from the New Hampshire border in a valley along Route 131 and near the areas of Hawkins Mountain and Proctor-Piper State Forest. The Phineas Gage Monument is a small, square stone located in a neat patch of grassy park area on the corner of Main Street and High Street, central between the post office, town building, and local volunteer fire department.

ALSO NEARBY

Tacos,Tacos! Authentic Mexican eats at 1 Lemere Square, off Route 103 (Main Street) in Ludlow, Vermont. Excellent food and excellent, friendly service!

Bennington Battle Monument

BENNINGTON, VERMONT

SITE HISTORY

There they are boys! We beat them today or Molly Stark sleeps a widow tonight!

—Brigadier General John Stark

August 16, 1777

In the late summer of 1777, Lieutenant General Burgoyne's British troops marched southward from Canada. His troops were badly in need of supplies, and they were 185 miles away from their nearest Canadian base and in serious trouble. They had been informed that nearby Bennington, Vermont, had a large supply of the necessities they had need of, and were under the impression that they would be easily gained from the large Loyalist population in the area— Burgoyne had been misinformed, and this error led to what would become a major turning point in the Revolutionary War.

Burgoyne told his troops, "the objective of your expedition is to try the affections of the country, to disconcert the councils of the enemy, to mount the Riedsel's dragoons, to complete Peter's Corps, and to obtain large supplies of cattle, horses, and carriages." He believed that the American militia had been scattered from Fort Ticonderoga but did not know that General John Stark had arrived with 500 reinforcements to join Colonel Seth Warner and the Vermont Militiamen.

Bennington Battle Monument.

Burgoyne sent a company under the helm of Lieutenant Colonel Friedrich Baum to form an encampment on a hill overlooking the Walloomsack River. On August 16, 1777, General Stark attacked the British forces from all sides. The Native Americans with the camp fled and the Loyalists scattered. The remaining forces fought until their ammunition was depleted, and then made a final sabre charge before Baum was mortally wounded and the troops were defeated.

Back at headquarters, General Burgoyne was irate—he had lost access to vital supplies, and his forces were now substantially depleted. He had no choice but to continue on toward Saratoga as is, a battle they handily lost, and this stunning defeat and Burgoyne's ultimate surrender turned the tide of the Revolutionary War.

The cornerstone for the Bennington Battle Monument was laid in 1887, with the monument being completed and dedicated in 1891. The 306-foot tower, the highest structure in Vermont, was built on the site of the coveted supplies. An elevator brings visitors to a viewing area at the top with stunning views of Vermont, Massachusetts, and New York. Annotated maps of the views help visitors spot locations such as the state house, Vermont Veterans Home, and local mountain ranges. Displays in the base of the monument feature dioramas of the military maneuvers and a kettle retrieved from Burgoyne's encampment. Twice a year visitors may elect to walk up the 427 stairs within the tower. Other memorials on the site include statues honoring Col. Seth Wagner and Brigadier General John Stark, and memorials to the military volunteers of all states that contributed in the Battle of Bennington—Vermont, New York, New Hampshire, and Massachusetts.

Statue of Brigadier General John Stark.

DIRECTIONS

The Bennington Battle Monument State Historic Site is located at 15 Monument Circle in Bennington, Vermont. Open mid-April to October 31 daily from 9:00 a.m. to 5:00 p.m. Admission is $5 for adults and $1 for children six to fourteen, and children under six are free. Free admission days are held annually on August 16, to commemorate the anniversary of the Bennington Battle, and on the second weekend of June for "Vermont Days," when all state historic sites offer free admission. Active military personnel and their immediate family members are admitted free at all times. Ample free parking is available, and the site is fully handicapped accessible.

ALSO NEARBY

The final resting place of famed New England poet Robert Frost can be found in the cemetery behind Old First Church, located at the corner of Monument Avenue and Church Lane in Bennington, Vermont.

The Bennington Triangle

BENNINGTON, VERMONT

SITE HISTORY

The "Bennington Triangle" is an area in southwestern Vermont that is shrouded in a great deal of mystery. Centered on Glastenbury Mountain in the Green Mountain National Forest, it includes all the towns that surround it, especially Bennington, Woodford, Shaftsbury, and Somerset. Local paranormal author Joseph A Citro coined the term to describe the area the local Native American tribes considered cursed by evil spirits, where the Four Winds met on the mountain. The woods, they believed, also harbored an enchanted stone that would swallow anyone unlucky enough to pass by. They feared the spirits and the monsters in the area would descend upon them if they entered for any reason other than to inter their dead in the tribal burial ground.

Similar to the Bermuda Triangle, the Bennington Triangle is reportedly a hotspot for UFO activity, strange lights and sounds, specters, and mysterious creatures, including Bigfoot sightings, hairy "wild men," and other strange beasts. Reports of the "Bennington Monster" have existed since the early nineteenth century. One local urban legend wildly told about the Sasquatch-like beast that occurred near Glastonbury. When a stagecoach was forced to stop due to a washed-out road, the driver noticed a footprint much too large to be human. When he turned to tell the occupants what he had spotted, a large, hairy creature suddenly attacked and knocked the carriage over with several blows. The passengers heard a deafening roar and only had time to glimpse a pair of glowing eyes before the beast rushed off into the darkness. It was last spotted in 2003, when Ray Dufresne of Winooski, Vermont, was driving by the mountain and saw what he told local reporters

Glastenbury Mountain, as seen from the top of the Bennington Battle Monument.

to be a large "black thing" by the road that was over six feet tall and "hairy from the top of his head to the bottom of his feet."

DOCUMENTED DISAPPEARANCES

Another similar coincidence between the Bennington and Bermuda Triangles is the number of mysterious and unsolved disappearances that have occurred within them. Between the years of 1945 and 1950 alone, five individuals met unexplained fates, and these cold cases still intrigue locals and visitors alike today;

MIDDIE RIVERS (1945)

On November 12, 1945, seventy-four-year-old Middie Rivers, an experienced local hunter and fisherman, disappeared while guiding a group of hunters up the mountain. On the way back to their camp at the end of the day, Rivers got ahead of the group a short ways in the vicinity of Long Trail Road and Route 9, vanished, and was never seen again. An extensive search was conducted but turned up only a single rifle shell in a nearby stream, possibly having dropped from Rivers's pocket while he was stopping for a drink. This disappearance was particularly perplexing because Rivers was very familiar with the area. No clue to his ultimate fate was ever uncovered.

PAULA WELDEN (1946)

On December 1, 1946, eighteen-year-old Bennington College sophomore Paula Welden had just finished a shift in the campus dining hall when she decided she was in the mood for a hike. She left at around 2:45 p.m., wearing a red coat with a fur collar, jeans, and sneakers. The weather was cold, and she seemed too lightly dressed for hiking, but many individuals spotted her in the vicinity of the Long Trail portion of the Appalachian Trail. After she received directions from a *Bennington Banner* employee, and a gas station owner noticed her running up the side of a gravel pit near the college entrance, a motorist picked up a hitchhiker matching her description and dropped her off at the Long Trail Trailhead parking lot.

She was confirmed to have made it onto the trail as well, since she was identified by a local elderly couple. While walking an estimated one hundred yards behind her, they watched her turn a corner in the trail and discovered that she'd vanished when they came around the same bend. When Welden did not return to her dorm room that evening, a search was quickly initiated by the local police force.

Previous attempts at establishing a state police force had been stymied by voters, and the Bennington Police Department was overwhelmed by the scope of the search. They called in resources from the Connecticut and New York State Police Departments, and later the FBI, but she did not turn up. Rumors swirled that she had left of her own volition to escape a family conflict, to live as a recluse on the mountain, or even to flee to Canada with an unnamed boyfriend, but not even a $5,000 reward put up by her father turned up any leads. The case was successful in convincing the public of the need for a Vermont State Police, however, and one was created in 1947, but no sign of Paula has ever surfaced.

JAMES TEDFORD (1949)

Exactly three years to the day after Welden's disappearance, James E. Tedford vanished from a full bus in broad daylight. Tedford was a resident of the Bennington Soldiers Home, now referred to as the Vermont Veterans Home, but had gone for a visit with family in St. Albans, Vermont, three hours away. It was on the return trip that fourteen other passengers claim to have seen him dozing in his seat when they hit Burlington, but by the time they pulled into the next station in Bennington he was inexplicably gone. His belongings were still in the luggage rack, and an opened bus schedule was in his vacant seat. Tedford's disappearance remains unsolved to this day.

PAUL JEPSON (1950)

The youngest victim of the Bennington Triangle was eight-year-old Paul Jepson. On October 12, 1950, Jepson accompanied his mother as she went about her duties as a caretaker at a local farm. His mother left him playing happily beside their truck, and when she reemerged from the pigsty, he had vanished. Search parties were immediately formed to find Paul, who like Paula Weldon had been wearing a red jacket that should have made spotting him easier. The state police bloodhounds tracked his scent to the nearby highway where Welden had been spotted hitchhiking, but then the trail went cold. No evidence was ever recovered, and Paul was never seen again.

FRIEDA LANGER (1950)

Just sixteen days after Paul Jepson vanished, fifty-three-year-old Frieda Langer met a similar fate. Langer and her cousin, Hebert Eisner, left their family campsite near the Somerset Reservoir to go on a hike. At some point in the excursion, Langer slipped and fell into a stream. Now cold and wet, she asked Eisner to wait for her while she quickly returned to camp to change her clothes. When Langer failed to return, Eisner made his way back to the site, where other family members told him she had not been seen since they had departed earlier.

Over the next two weeks, 300 police and fire department staff, civilian volunteers, and military members conducted inch-by-inch searches both by ground and air. The searches marked the first time a helicopter had been used to aid a search-and-recovery mission in Vermont history. No trace of Frieda was found in any of those searches.

On May 12, 1951, her body was discovered near the Somerset Reservoir in an area that had been extensively searched multiple times seven months previously. She was wearing the same clothes she had been wearing when she had disappeared. Her body appeared to have been exposed to the elements and was so badly decomposed that no cause of death could be determined. Langer was the last of the rash of disappearances, and the only one whose body was recovered.

AUTHOR'S NOTE

Since the Long Trail featured prominently in several disappearances, I decided I wanted to attempt to retrace Paula Welden's hike into the Green Mountain National Forest. Leaving Sandra in the parking lot nursing a sore knee, I made my way to the trailhead. Though the parking lot had been full, and someone had left a cache of supplies for hikers in need (presumably those hiking the 2,200-mile Appalachian Trail from end to end), there was not a soul in sight. I followed the trail along a stream and curved around multiple bends for about half a mile before I became a bit spooked. Despite the dense forest surrounding me, I heard no animals and the woods were an almost unnatural quiet. With tales of unsolved disappearances in mind, I turned back on the trail. Whether a result of alien abductions, monster attacks, serial killers, or even a man-eating rock, I was not eager to join the ranks. When I turned the final corner and returned to our vehicle, Sandra was visibly relieved. I had been gone just long enough to set her own imagination on fire.—S. P.

DIRECTIONS

The 272-mile-long Long Trail portion of the Appalachian Trail runs the length of Vermont and crosses the summit of Glastenbury Mountain. It is best accessed through the trailhead on Route 9 between Bennington and Wilmington, just east of the Walloomsac Brook. Parking is available in a small lot on the north side of the highway.

Glastenbury Mountain is also visible from the top of the Bennington Battle Monument at 15 Monument Circle in Bennington, Vermont.

The Vermont Veterans Home is located at 325 North Street in Bennington. It features several monuments to fallen soldiers from different wars and conflicts.

Grave of Madame Sherri

BRATTLEBORO, VERMONT

The famed Parisian-born performer Antoinette Bremare, more famously known as just Madame Sherri, rests in peace beneath a simple stone at Meetinghouse Cemetery in Brattleboro, Vermont. Read more about her colorful life and see the stunning stone castle she called home in New Hampshire in chapter 13.

SITE INFORMATION

Madame Sherri's final resting spot is located at Meetinghouse Hill Cemetery in Brattleboro, Vermont. When entering the cemetery from the Orchard Street gate, follow the main road. Take your second left. You should be able to spot the large George family plot right at this corner. You will come to an intersection and make a quick right. Half of the way down this road on the left is a small one-by-two-foot bronze plaque labeled "Antoinette Sherri, 1876–1965." Though it is raised slightly off the ground, it is not readable from a distance.

Madame Sherri's grave.

DIRECTIONS

Meetinghouse Hill Cemetery is located on Orchard Street in Brattleboro, Vermont.

ALSO NEARBY

For excellent lunch and dinner options, try Ramunto's Brick Oven Pizza at 1111 Putney Road in Brattleboro, Vermont. Portion sizes are ample, and their pizza, salads, pastas, and garlic knots are delicious.

Betty and Barney Hill's Alien Abduction

LINCOLN AND KINGSTON, NEW HAMPSHIRE

SITE HISTORY

The incident known as the "Hills' Abduction" or the "Zeta Reticuli Incident" took place on the overnight of September 19–20, 1961, involving Betty and Barney Hill near the Profile Rock area of US Route 3 in the White Mountains of New Hampshire. It is a well-researched and well-documented incident that has been much recounted in countless print and film coverage of the event—the most celebrated of these being the book *Interrupted Journey*, by John G. Fuller, and the made-for-TV movie *The UFO Incident* in 1975.

The Hills, a respected biracial couple from Portsmouth, New Hampshire, were riding in their 1957 Chevy Bel Air on a return trip home from a vacation to Canada when they were reportedly chased and abducted by extraterrestrial beings in a UFO. The incident was reported the day after arriving home, when the Hills put together their clues and recollections of their experience, which included two hours of unexplained "missing" time during their trip. They came to the strange and frightening conclusion that what they had experienced was an alien abduction.

The Hills claimed to have been taken aboard a spacecraft, where they were poked and prodded by alien beings as the subjects of scientific experiments and were able to communicate with these beings through telepathic dialogue during the event. Later, Betty Hill, with the help of an amateur astronomer, created a controversial star map that pinpointed the origination of these alien beings as coming from the Zeta Reticuli star system.

The detailed investigation, review of evidence, and reconstruction of the event that followed soon painted a clear picture that something extraordinary had indeed happened to Betty and Barney Hill. This incident was validated by multiple leaders in varied

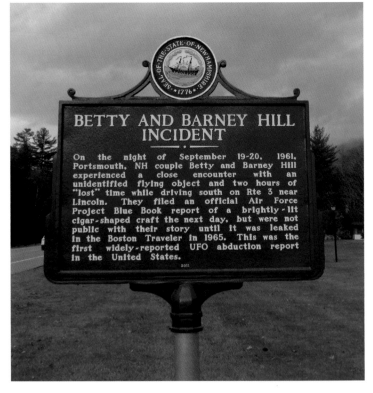

The highway marker on US Route 3, near the Indian Head Resort.

fields of research. Dr. Benjamin Simon, a well-known Boston psychiatrist, carefully conducted individual hypnosis sessions with the Hills, from which repressed details of the abduction were recalled. Dr. Stanton Friedman, an award-winning nuclear physicist and lead civilian investigator on the 1947 Roswell Incident in New Mexico, also collected evidence and researched the event with the Hills; he discovered many similarities between the cases and later

Top left: Profile Rock. Top right and bottom left: Indian Head Resort.

published prolifically about it. Finally, the National Investigations Committee on Aerial Phenomena (NICAP) conducted extensive interviews with the Hills. All these field experts concluded that Betty and Barney Hill had indeed experienced exactly what they had reported.

To further substantiate their recounting of the time and events, the Hills obtained the official radar report from nearby Pease Air Force Base, which indicated that the base had tracked an unidentified aircraft at approximately 2:14 a.m. on September 20, 1961, near the time and location the Hills reported the UFO had dropped them off at the end of their abduction experience. The Hills' incident is the first to be publicly acknowledged and recognized by a state government, with the state of New Hampshire erecting a memorial plaque along US Route 3 in Lincoln, New Hampshire. Abundant research materials from the case, including the now-declassified CIA and FBI documents and original Air Force intelligence reports, can be found in the special-collection archive of the Betty and Barney Hill Papers 1961–2006, which is housed at the University of New Hampshire Library, Betty's alma mater. Everything from the dress Betty was wearing at the time of the abduction, to their handwritten journals and drawings of the craft and the alien beings, are protected within the archives for future researchers and scholars of UFO activity.

AUTHOR'S NOTE

The drive along Highway 3 through the White Mountains of New Hampshire is a pretty lonely one during a routine, nonholiday weekend. The day that we decided to travel through the area, there was not a lot of traffic until arriving at the exit where the Hills' official memorial to the incident is located. There are very few highway lights or streetlights along the way, which provides ample darkness to see the sky and the stars in it very clearly, but also makes the road and surrounding woods seem overwhelmingly black and ominous. This area's high-up clouds seem mysterious, surrounded by large mountains and blasted rock on both sides of the highway, with nothing and no one else around.

I can imagine how it was back in the fall of 1961, when Betty and Barney drove through this area with even fewer cars and buildings than are currently present. It must have been extra dark that night and have seemed even more eerie to be lone travelers on the road. The area does hold a strange sensation of being utterly alone but not lonely, if you know what I mean. We pulled over a couple of times to check our location on the map, and I kept feeling spooked by a feeling that something was watching us from the woods along the dark road.

We later made a visit to the Hills' final resting place at Greenwood Cemetery in Kingston, New Hampshire. The feeling at this site was sharply different in tone and was very peaceful, seeming to be protected by positive energy and positive spirits. We chuckled at the *Toy Story* alien toy left in tribute at the gravesite, and we couldn't help but wonder what the Hills would have thought of the cutesy depiction of alien beings. —S. G.

Final resting place of Betty and Barney Hill.

DIRECTIONS

The site of Betty and Barney Hill's abduction is located just south of Profile Rock and the Indian Head Resort on US Route 3 in Lincoln, New Hampshire. The New Hampshire state plaque dedicating the spot is easily reached by parking in the resort's parking lot and walking toward the Native American teepee and totem pole. The resort has been open since 1913 and offers traditional rooms, cottages, and private house rentals, as well as ample dining options, an observation tower, and a large gift shop. Many music and special events are held year-round at the resort, including a popular psychic fair every November and April. Reservations for lodging, dining, and events can be made by visiting www.indianheadresort.com or calling 1-800-343-8000.

The final resting place of the Hills is at Greenwood Cemetery off North Road in Kingston, New Hampshire. When you enter the main gate, drive toward the rear of the cemetery as far as you can go and then head right. The couple is buried beneath a gray tombstone engraved with the names Barney Hill and Eunice Barrett, Betty's maiden name. Plaques along the ground remind visitors of their "Interrupted Journey."

The *Challenger* Explosion

CONCORD, NEW HAMPSHIRE

SITE HISTORY

We will never forget them, nor the last time we saw them, this morning as they prepared for their journey and waved goodbye and slipped the surly bonds of Earth to touch the face of God.

—President Ronald Reagan
National TV address, Jan. 28, 1986

On January 28, 1986, seventy-three seconds into its flight, space shuttle *Challenger*, on mission STS-51-L, exploded, which resulted in the deaths of all seven crew members: five NASA astronauts and two payload specialists, including Francis R. Scobee, Michael J. Smith, Ellison S. Onizuka, Judith A. Resnik, Ronald E. McNair, Gregory B. Jarvis, and S. Christa McAuliffe. Originally set to launch on January 22, a series of delays to the previous mission (STS-61-C) and inclement weather both at Cape Canaveral and at the Transoceanic Abort Landing site in Senegal pushed the launch to its fateful date.

At 11:39 a.m. EST the *Challenger* launched, and almost immediately thereafter an O-ring seal in the right solid rocket booster (SRB) failed. These O-rings were not designed to be used in temperatures such as the unusually cold twenty-eight degrees that day, and this resulted in a failure of the O-ring to seal properly. Its failure caused a breach in the SRB joint it should have sealed, allowing pressurized burning gas from within the solid rocket motor to reach the external fuel tank, which then suffered a complete structural failure, and a fireball engulfed the whole stack.

The gate to Calvary Cemetery in Concord, New Hampshire.

The crew compartment fell in one piece and slowly tumbled in a ballistic arc to the sea surface. Though the precise timing of the deaths is not exactly known, it is clear that at least three of the crew survived the initial breakup of the spacecraft, because they had activated Personal Egress Air Packs on the flight deck. Since they were protected by lever locks that needed to be pulled against a spring, and the force of disintegration of the ocean impact would have been sufficient to disengage them, this was accepted as evidence of their survival of the initial event. There was no escape system equipped, and the impact of the crew compartment with the ocean at 207 mph was too violent to be survivable.

A lengthy search-and-recovery mission immediately began, and on March 7, the crew compartment and some vehicle fragments were discovered on the ocean floor. Unfortunately, the remains of the crew were in poor condition due to the prolonged exposure to the salt water. Resnik, McAuliffe, and additional unidentifiable remains were recovered over the next few hours. During their recovery, Jarvis's body floated away from divers multiple times. Though autopsies were performed, due to the condition of the remains, no exact cause of death was able to be determined.

On April 29, seven hearses picked up seven identical coffins, each draped with an American flag, which were carried past an honor guard and were followed by an astronaut escort. They were flown to Dover Air Force Base in Delaware and were then processed and released to relatives. Resnik, Scobee, and Captain Smith were interred in individual graves at Arlington National Cemetery near a memorial in which the unidentified remains were communally buried. Onizuka was interred in Honolulu, Hawaii, and McAuliffe was returned to her hometown of Concord, New Hampshire, not far from the high school in which she taught social studies.

It is Christa McAuliffe who is the loss most well remembered of the *Challenger* seven. She had been selected from more than 11,000 applicants to participate in the NASA Teacher in Space Project. She wrote in her application, "I watched the Space Age being born, and I want to participate." She was an immediate media sensation, even appearing on *Good Morning America* and the *Tonight Show with Johnny Carson*, and it has been estimated that seventeen percent of Americans, including many school children, were watching live solely to see McAuliffe become the first

McAuliffe's tombstone.

teacher in space, and within an hour eighty-five percent of Americans were aware of the tragedy.

She was honored after her death with the 2004 Congressional Space Medal of Honor, and many education centers were named after her including the McAuliffe-Shepard Discovery Center and the Christa Corrigan McAuliffe Center for Education and Teaching Excellence at Framingham State University, her alma mater. Besides over forty schools around the world, asteroid 3352 and craters both on the moon and Venus were named in her honor.

The McAuliffe-Shepard Discovery Center, named both after Christa and Alan Shepard (a fellow Granite State astronaut, the first American in space, and one of only twelve people to have walked on the moon), is a popular spot for school field trips and tourist visits. The 45,000-square-foot center features interactive science and engineering exhibits, a full-dome digital planetarium, an observatory, a science store, and a café. Hours and exhibitions vary by season, but it is well worth the meager price of admission for all ages.

AUTHOR'S NOTE

As a child growing up in Manchester, New Hampshire, I will never forget this tragic moment in aerospace history. It was two days before my eighth birthday, and since we lived so close to where Christa McAuliffe was teaching, we were part of the seventeen percent watching live with great pomp and circumstance. We had been learning about space and NASA for weeks and were eagerly anticipating participating in the experiments and lessons she would teach from space. We had made decorations and signs and had crammed ourselves into the classroom next door and screamed the countdown at the top of our lungs.

I distinctly remember seeing that bright flash of light and had just enough time to wonder if it was supposed to happen before my teacher burst into tears. Even at that age, it was alarming to see all of the adults so shaken all at once, and it was instantly clear to us all that something very, very bad had happened. The principal startled us all by suddenly coming onto the intercom and asking us all to return to our classrooms. It was a moment that, even thirty years later, remains so vivid in my memory, and visiting her final resting place was incredibly moving for me. As a career educator myself, she will always stand out as an inspiration to us all, and I hope more people find time to stop by and pay their respects. —S. P.

DIRECTIONS

Christa McAuliffe is buried at Calvary Cemetery on North Main Street in Concord, New Hampshire. Her large granite marker sits high on the hill at the rear of the cemetery, overlooking the city where she taught. The inscription on her stone reads:

S. Christa McAuliffe
September 2, 1948–January 28, 1986

Wife mother teacher
PIONEER WOMAN
Crew member, space shuttle Challenger
America's first ordinary citizen to
venture toward space

She helped people. She laughed. She loved and is loved. She appreciated the world's natural beauty. She was curious and sought to learn who we are and what the universe is about. She relied on her own judgment and moral courage to do right. She cared about the suffering of her fellow man. She tried to protect our spaceship Earth. She taught her children to do the same.

The McAuliffe-Shepard Discovery Center is located at 2 Institute Drive in Concord, New Hampshire. Its hours vary from season to season and should be checked by calling 603-271-7827 or visiting www.starhop.com. The center is handicapped accessible and parking is free.

Smuttynose Murders

PORTSMOUTH, NEW HAMPSHIRE

SITE HISTORY

Do I look like a man who would commit
such a crime?
—Louis Wagner

You look to me like a man that got himself into
a corner and murdered his way out.
—Governor Nelson Dingley

On the Isles of Shoals, the series of tiny islands scattered along the Maine and New Hampshire border, fishing has always been a way of life. It was a call to the sea that led Maren and John Hontvet to purchase a small red house on Smuttynose Island. The recent immigrants from Norway had originally settled in Boston but had disliked city life. John purchased a fishing schooner, named it the *Clara Bella*, and was able to turn enough of a profit that enabled the Hontvets not only to enjoy a comfortable existence but even to bring Maren's sister, Karen Christensen, from Norway to join them.

Business was going so well that in the spring of 1872, John offered a job to assist him to Louis Wagner, a Prussian immigrant living in nearby Portsmouth, New Hampshire, in exchange for room and board in the Hontvets' workshop. Though he would have preferred to be paid outright, he did enjoy the stability of the living arrangement and having Maren providing all his cooking and cleaning.

The sisters-in-law sleep side by side for eternity.

That fall brought more family from Norway, as Maren and Karen's brother, Ivan, and his new bride, Anethe, joined them on the island. Due to being joined by another able-bodied man, and Wagner's increasing bouts of rheumatism, his arrangements with the Hontvets ended soon thereafter, and he returned to Portsmouth.

The winter of 1873 had been a harsh one, but business continued as usual. The women were frequently left alone on the island while their husbands were away fishing, and the evening of March 5 was no different. John and Ican had taken the *Clara Bella* to Portsmouth to pick up a shipment of bait. When the shipment was delayed, word was sent to Maren that they would not be returning until the following day. The men ran into Wagner and offered him a job loading the bait. He knew they weren't returning to the island that night, and when the pair arrived the following morning, he was nowhere to be found.

THE CRIMES

Around 8:00 p.m. that evening, a rowboat was stolen from Pickering Wharf in Portsmouth. The thief rowed hours across miles of open sea and docked on the south side of the island. He walked through the snow and directly to the only occupied house on the island—the Hontvets'. The women were bunked downstairs: Karen, who there visiting her sister, was in a makeshift bed in the kitchen, and Maren and Anethe were in a nearby bedroom, when the front door creaked open. It alerted Ringe, the family dog, whose barking awoke Karen. Startled to discover someone in the kitchen, the intruder hastily grabbed a chair and hit Karen with it repeatedly. Thinking it was her brother-in-law returned from the sea, she cried out, "John is killing me! John is killing me!"

Woken by her sister's screams, Maren opened the bedroom door to find the shadow of a man beating Karen. When he paused in his attack, Maren hastily pulled her into the bedroom and bolted the door. Enraged, the man started beating down the door, and Maren quickly realized their only means of escape was out the window.

Maren screamed for Anethe to run, and though she did clamber out the window, fear overtook her and she froze in terror a few feet outside the building. The man burst out the front door, grabbed a nearby ax for chopping wood and ice, and ran at her. In the moonlight his face was exposed and as Maren watched in horror, Wagner raised the ax and crushed Anethe's skull will a single blow. She had just enough time to scream her last words—"Louis! Louis! Louis!"

Knowing he had been recognized, Wagner returned inside and continued trying to break down the bedroom door. Maren realized that it was only a matter of time before he made his way in, and since Karen was close to death, she needed to leave her behind. Just as she threw her legs over the edge, Wagner burst through the door. She jumped just as he swung the ax, hitting the sill with such force that the handle broke off.

She heard Karen scream as Wagner finished her off; Maren bolted for the dock on the north side of the island, planning to take Wagner's boat to make her escape. Finding the dock empty, she hastily grabbed Ringe to keep him from barking and giving her location away. She hid herself on an isolated section of rock. Barefoot in her nightclothes, with only the dog to keep her warm, Maren stayed hidden until dawn. She then ran along a small breakwater to Malaga Island, where she was able to get the attention of some children playing on nearby Appledore Island.

The morning after the crime, Wagner was spotted eating breakfast at a boardinghouse, looking haggard and like he hadn't slept. He caught the 9:00 a.m. train to Boston, where he bought a new suit and boots, cut his hair, and shaved his beard. Meanwhile, Maren had reported the crimes, and a manhunt had begun. Wagner made a mistake when he returned to the North End neighborhood he had once lived in, and he was quickly recognized. By 7:00 p.m. that very night he had been arrested and was on the train back to Portsmouth. When he arrived at the station, over 500 angry townspeople were waiting and shadowed him all the way to the police station, chanting, "Lynch him! Kill him!"

Though closer to the New Hampshire coastline, the island is technically a part of Maine and he had to be extradited to Alfred, Maine, to await his day in court. During the transfer, a lynch mob of over 200 local lobstermen threw rocks and bricks at the prisoner and his escort of revolver-toting officers and bayonet-wielding Marines.

THE TRIAL

On June 9, 1873, the nine-day trial of Louis Wagner commenced. The prosecuting attorney delivered a strong case, including not only Maren's eyewitness testimony but also substantial circumstantial evidence. After Wagner's arrest, it was discovered that he had hidden a bloody shirt in the boardinghouse privy, that the exact amount stolen from the house had been spent on his new outfit, and that he had known the women were alone in the house with the cash John had been saving for a new boat. Probably most damning, when Wagner was arrested, he had one of Maren's buttons nestled among the change in his pocket.

Wagner didn't help his own case, by giving rambling and sometimes incoherent testimony. Though he steadfastly proclaimed his innocence, his alibis did not check out. He initially claimed that he had been working that night baiting trawls on a fishing boat, but he couldn't name the boat, its captain, or what pier it had been docked at. He also claimed to have gone to a saloon and had two beers but couldn't name the saloon or its location, and no witnesses supported his claim.

He was found guilty of premeditated murder and sentenced to death. That very night, Wagner picked the lock of his cell with the end of a wooden toothbrush and escaped to New Hampshire when the guard took his 3:00 a.m. break. He was recaptured by a group of vigilantes and met his ends at the gallows at Thomaston, Maine, as one of the final five men executed before the state abolished capital punishment.

DIRECTIONS

Smuttynose Island welcomes day visitors during the summer months. The island is reachable by rowboat or dinghy, which can be tied up in the harbor. Walking tours are available, but no public restroom facilities are available. The Isles of Shoals can be viewed by sea through many regularly scheduled tours through the Isles of Shoals Steamship Company (visit www.islesofshoals.com).

The final resting place of Karen and Anethe Christensen is at South Cemetery, at the corner of South Street and Sagamore Avenue in Portsmouth, New Hampshire. Their stones bear the matching epitaphs, "A sudden death, A striking call, A warning voice that speaks to all, To all to be prepared to die." To find their stones, find the tombstone of James M. Pickering along the wall along Sagamore Avenue. Take the grassy path to the left of it, and the Christensens' matching graves are on the left facing the path a few hundred feet down.

South Cemetery.

Madame Sherri's Castle

CHESTERFIELD, NEW HAMPSHIRE

SITE HISTORY

Madame Sherri, born Antoinette Bremare, in Paris, France, in 1878, was a noted performer on the Paris music hall scene. After meeting, falling in love with, and marrying an American silent-film performer by the name of Andre Riela, the duo took the White Star oceanic line to the United States. Upon arriving in New York City, they began new careers and rebranded themselves as renowned dancers and costume designers on Broadway and with the Ziegfeld Follies.

Known to be quite the partyers, the Sherris enjoyed the bustling New York City nightlife, despite the onset of Prohibition. They enjoyed throwing lavish parties with their fellow performers, and gin and other spirits were flowing plentifully. Unfortunately, in-dulgent party behaviors were the demise of Andre, and in 1924, he went blind and reportedly insane before dying at the Manhattan State Hospital. Though the official cause of death was noted as "general paralysis of the insane," the word that passed among his friends and acquaintances was that an illness due to complications of venereal disease and the effects of bathtub gin directly caused his passing.

To say that Madame Sherri took his death poorly would be an understatement. Andre had been the love of her life, and the glitzy nightlife in the city no longer appealed to her. She started sum-mering in New Hampshire and, after visiting the small rural town of Chesterfield, purchased a small farm. Over the next few years, she added acreage to the farm, and sometime between 1929 and 1932, Madame Sherri commissioned a French-style chateau that she referred to as her castle. She was heavily involved in every aspect of the construction, frequently hovering and critiquing builders' efforts. Many became so frustrated that they quit, and, as a result, there were some significant construction delays.

The remains of the grand staircase to the second floor of Madame Sherri's Castle.

When the project was completed, Madame Sherri's castle featured a cozy little bistro with six red-tableclothed tables in the basement, and a main floor with a huge bar that you entered between two enormous trees growing right through the roof. A massive second-story balcony sat below a third floor that held Madame's living quarters, which were accessible from a large exterior stone staircase. Also on the property were the beautiful Indian Pond and

NEW HAMPSHIRE

a man-made swimming pond with a statue of Aphrodite in the center of it, which Madame and her guests delighted in skinny-dipping in.

Madame Sherri's eccentricities and flamboyant nature made her a hot topic of gossip in Chesterfield. The scandals she caused in the quiet New Hampshire town were only amplified by her fondness of being driven into town in her cream-colored 1927 Packard automobile, wearing her long fur coat with nothing underneath it. People seemed particularly annoyed by her penchant for arriving in town with her pet monkey perched on her shoulder. With the rumors of her parties involving illegal liquor and many unwed men and women from the city, some of the locals even went so far as to question if she was a bona fide madame.

After years of lavish parties, her money ran dry, and the castle exceeded Madame's resources. She eventually moved to the Maple Rest Home in nearby Brattleboro, Vermont. She lived out the rest of her years as a ward of the state and in near-destitute conditions.

In 1962 the castle burned to the ground, and authorities were unable to officially determine whether the fire was an accidental bonfire or the result of arson, since many in the community were bothered by watching the home slowly fall apart. Today, the grand stone staircase, the basement bistro, and the foundation are a popular backdrop for photo sheets and beautiful hiking trails.

Many paranormal enthusiasts have investigated the grounds with good success, often hearing the sounds of music and party revelry. Several individuals have observed a full-body apparition of Madame Sherri in elaborate dress slowly descending the stone staircase to greet you as her guest.

AUTHOR'S NOTE

We had previously visited the castle and felt that there was a lot of positive energy at the location. Since there were minimal other visitors when we first arrived, we decided to try to make contact with any lingering spirits in the area. After we appeared to make contact with an intelligent and curious male spirit that was within the basement bistro area, we invited it to escort us down to our vehicle and attempted to make contact with a Ghost Box session.

This was a very successful session with many instances of direct and relevant responses to our questions, both of our names and several brief responses in French. The full video of this investigation with annotated audio is available at our YouTube channel at www.youtube.com/ScaryNewEngland. —S. P.

DIRECTIONS

Madame Sherri's Forest is on Gulf Road in Chesterfield, New Hampshire. It is accessed through a red steel gate, and there is parking available for up to a dozen vehicles. Well-mannered dogs are permitted on leashes.

ALSO NEARBY

The Society for the Protection of New Hampshire Forests maintains several well-marked trails through the Madame Sherri Forest:

Indian Pond Trail—an easy forty-five-minute round-trip hike to the secluded and beautiful mountain lake.

Ann Stokes Loop—a two-mile, one-and-a-half-hour hike with varied terrain that provides great views Chesterfield and Indian Pond.

Daniels Mountain Loop—a 1.8-mile, one-and-a-half-hour hike over moderate terrain with occasional steep sections that leads to the summit of Daniels Mountain and great views of East Hill and Moon Ledge.

Daniels Mountain Trail—a forty-five-minute hike crossing streams and passing stone walls through a forest of moss and hemlocks

Also, see page 36, for information about visiting Madame Sherri's final resting place in nearby Brattleboro, Vermont.

The Murder of Gregg Smart

DERRY, NEW HAMPSHIRE

SITE HISTORY

This sensational story put Rockingham County, New Hampshire, on the newsworthy map and highlighted a mix of the loss of teenage innocence and media sensationalism. The case involved twenty-two-year-old Pamela Smart, media coordinator at Winnacunnet High School in Hampton, New Hampshire, who seemed to strategically have an affair with an impressionable fifteen-year-old high school student, William "Billy" Flynn, and convinced him to conspire in the murder of her husband. The tragic event took place on May 1, 1990, in Derry, New Hampshire, where twenty-four-year-old Gregg Smart was ambushed, attacked, and unapologetically murdered by gunshot to the head in the condo that he shared with his wife, Pamela.

This particular case is embedded in many a New Englander's memory, since it was the first legal proceeding in the northern area to be openly televised and broadcast across the nation. Arrested for the crime along with Pamela Smart and Billy Flynn were Billy's friends and alleged coconspirators Patrick "Pete" Randall, Vance "J. R." Lattime Jr., Raymond Fowler, and Cecilia Pierce. On March 22, 1991, Pamela Smart was found guilty of conspiracy to commit murder, witness tampering, and accomplice to first-degree murder and was sentenced to life in prison without parole.

Since then, there have been multiple pop culture news articles, books, movies, television episodes, prison interviews, and documentaries based on the case. There are equal amounts of movies and publications persuading audiences of her guilt or innocence. The most compelling evidence against Pamela Smart was documented at her trial and lives on in footage that you can find posted

The condo of Gregg and Pamela Smart in Derry, New Hampshire.

NEW HAMPSHIRE

on YouTube and various documentaries. As a counterpoint, there is also a website dedicated to supporting the innocence of Pamela Smart (www.pamelasmart.com), which has a link to documents highlighting facts about the case in her favor and her many "achievements" while in prison. It also notes her as the victim being unfairly treated as a "Scarlet Prisoner." The latest documentary, titled *Captivated: The Trials of Pamela Smart*, directed by Jeremiah Zagar and exclusively released by HBO in 2014, questions her conviction by reason of wrongful damnation in the media and bias, and possible evidence tampering with information presented by the prosecution, causing an unfair trial.

Another interesting aspect of the story is how an older, manipulating teacher figure is able to take hold of an impressionable youth with an undeveloped mind to commit such acts of desperation on her behalf. It took mere months, after bonding through a mutual interest in heavy-metal music, for young Billy Flynn to start having sex with Pamela and to be convinced to go forward with planning and carrying out the murder of Gregg.

Recent developments in the case included renewed media attention when William "Billy" Flynn was released on parole from Maine State Prison in Warren, Maine, in June 2015. It is reported that he successfully completed a continuing-education program, various counseling programs, and a work-release program and had a meaningful relationship with a woman from the area. He has chosen to stay in Maine and wishes to stay out of the public eye in an effort to lead a quiet life for the remainder of his days.

The year 2015 also marked twenty-five years in prison for Pamela Smart. From the start, Pamela has claimed her innocence but has also made multiple incriminating statements during recorded telephone conversations with Cecilia Pierce, another one of her students. Her current narrative also continues to hold conflicting statements against the evidence. She is the only one who does not admit any wrongdoing, except having an affair with Billy Flynn, and today she is the only one who remains in prison with no chance of parole.

AUTHOR'S NOTE

To honor the memory and acknowledge the loss of the victim, Gregg Smart, we made a visit to his burial site at Forest Hill Cemetery, East Derry, New Hampshire. In the rear of the cemetery, Gregg lies at rest with his mother and father, who joined him there in 1998 and 2010, respectively. The small stone is adorned with a heart, and from the number of stones and trinkets left at the stone, it is one of the most visited in the cemetery. It was a shock for me to discover that my own grandparents, Arlamae and Francis Paradis, were buried so close to the Smart family plot. My niece, Ashlee Tufo, and I took the time to clean up both plots and wished them both peace. —S. P.

DIRECTIONS

The crime scene is located in condo 4E on Misty Morning Drive in Derry, New Hampshire. The sensational trial was held at Rockingham County Court, 10 New Hampshire-125, in Brentwood, New Hampshire, The final resting place of Gregg Smart is located at Forest Hill Cemetery, East Derry, New Hampshire. His stone can be found by driving through the main gates and driving straight to the rear, with the Smart family plot located to the left of the main roadway.

Gregg Smart's headstone and Forest Hill Cemetery gates.

America's Stonehenge

SALEM, NEW HAMPSHIRE

SITE HISTORY

You've probably heard of the collection of megaliths in England, but did you know that America has its own version of Stonehenge located in New England? Our take on this prehistoric archaeological enigma is located in Salem, New Hampshire. Opened to the public in 1958 under the name of the "Mystery Hill Caves," it has been operated under its current title of "America's Stonehenge" by the aptly named Stone family since 1982.

After watching a brief video and picking up a self-guided tour map, guests explore the thirty-acre site along a half- to one-mile gradually inclining hike over an uneven rock terrain. Along the way, signs, fences, and numbered plaques point out thirty-two points of interest, including a Sundeck Chamber, a Sacrificial Table, and an Oracle Chamber, as well as cairns, monoliths, and suspected encampments or farms. Additionally, an astronomical chart in the center of a raised and covered wooden tower guides visitors to view huge upright stones hundreds of feet away in the surrounding forest. These stones fashion a giant astronomically aligned calendar that appears to coincide with events such as the Summer Solstice, Vernal Equinox, Samhain, and Yule.

The nine-by-six-foot Sacrificial Table, with its notched drainage tract around the circumference to drain the "blood" away, is propped up on four stone legs. It sits directly on top of the Oracle Chamber, from which a tube funnels voices from below that appear to emanate from the Sacrificial Table itself. This feature was allegedly used as part of ceremonies to suggest that a disembodied

Intricately arranged stones at America's Stonehenge.

voice or spirit had been conjured. (Try it yourself when you visit—the voice echoing up the chamber does take on a decidedly supernatural quality!)

How the alignment of these stones and the structures came to be is a topic of debate. The Stone family asserts that they have documentation of carbon dating of the stones from 4,000 years ago, with a single fire pit 7,300 years old. They point out that the stones bear the markings of Stone Age technology with its stone-on-stone etching, rather than Metal Age technology. They also are quick to showcase markings on stones that they believe resemble Ogham, Phoenician, and Iberian Punic scripts.

The earliest documented use of the site was as the homestead of Jonathan Pattee. The Pattee family farmed in the area in 1823 and used the stone grottoes for food and crop storage. The creation of the Sacrificial Table could also have been tied to this time period, with similar tables having been used as apple presses in cider production and lye leaching in soapmaking.

Many rumors about the property, including undocumented reports that the caves were used as a stop on the Underground Railroad and that H. P. Lovecraft was inspired by them, after viewing the Sacrificial Table, to create the stone circle atop the Sentinel Hill setting in *The Dunwich Horror*. Some people report that they have experienced paranormal events and gathered evidence of a haunting at the site, and several times per year local paranormal groups host public ghost-hunting expeditions on the site. Evidence generated on these investigations is on display in the visitor center.

Anthropologists and archaeologists who have researched the site have not found any significant relics of the Bronze Age. Though they hypothesize that the structures could have been created by a Native American or the early migrant European population, the man-made structures would have had to be crafted by someone decidedly well versed in stone construction and astronomy.

The true origins of the former "Mystery Hills" may be difficult to figure out. At best, it is a location of historical significance as one of the oldest settlements in New England, or its strange "script-like" markings may be a result of having been moved to benefit its modern use as a tourist attraction. What is to be sure is that it is made of rocks and is older than anyone alive.

The Visitor Center at America's Stonehenge.

DIRECTIONS

America's Stonehenge is located at 105 Haverhill Road in Salem, New Hampshire. Plenty of free on-site parking is available, but due to the uneven terrain, it is not handicapped accessible. Though the site is very family friendly, due to the presence of alpacas that call the site home, animals are not permitted. Though you may exercise dogs in the lower parking lot, leaving them in your vehicle is discouraged.

America's Stonehenge is open to the public year-round, with access to many acres of groomed snowshoeing trails in the winter and occasional paranormal investigations and special events held on astronomical holidays such as the equinoxes. Details on special events can be found at www.stonehengeusa.com.

ALSO NEARBY

When in the area, stopping by Stachey's Olde-Time Pizzeria at 517 South Broadway is a must. In addition to their fantastic pizza offerings, their chicken teriyaki salad served with homemade pita pocket bread is hard to beat, and we consider ourselves connoisseurs of grilled chicken salads! View their hours and menu at www.stacheys.com

Gilson Cemetery

NASHUA, NEW HAMPSHIRE

SITE HISTORY

When a plot of land dates back to precolonial times, records are difficult to maintain, and urban legends rise to fill in the gaps. Such is the case with a small, 500-by-150-foot tract of land that became a cemetery in Nashua, New Hampshire.

The cemetery is reportedly one of the most haunted locations in the entire Granite State. In addition to an ominous and oppressive force that seeks to keep intruders from entering the grounds, visitors and passersby have reported light anomalies, orbs shooting from the ground toward the sky, streaks of light and color, voices, and far-off battle cries. Many full-bodied apparitions have also been seen on the grounds, most notably a lady in white who walks between the graves, frequently from an area of suspected unmarked graves toward, and disappearing into, a stone wall at the rear of the cemetery.

Paranormal groups who have investigated the grounds have reported the usual smattering of electronic voice phenomena, photographs, and videos of orbs and shadow people, electromagnetic field (EMF) fluctuations, equipment and camera malfunctions, and severe battery drainage. A phantom biker has been recounted as regularly riding past the cemetery, as well as watchers in colonial-era clothing in the woods to the rear, who appear to be monitoring what is going on in the grounds. Notable spikes in the levels of observable paranormal activity have been reported.

The grave of Joseph W. Gilson.

NEW HAMPSHIRE

Gilson Cemetery wall.

Many of the legends in the cemetery seem to have their genesis in bloody Native American battles reportedly waged on the very spot where the cemetery sits. History does indicate that rival tribes came to blows in Dunstable, the original name of the town, though historians have alternatively suggested that it may have been the Penacook versus the Mohawk tribes and the northern Penobscot tribes versus the southern tribes of Massachusetts and Rhode Island. Regardless of which tribes were the participants, it is a certainty that native blood was shed in the area and that many of those who passed away may have been offended by the land later being commandeered for use as a final resting spot for "the white man."

A popular local legend also tells the tale of a medicine man who went mad and was banished to the area. He would lure the young men of the tribe to their demise with the promise of being anointed with greater power and more strength than their peers. In doing so, the medicine man prolonged his own life by sacrificing them to dark spirits. One day he made the wrong decision, and one of the young men ultimately overpowered and slayed him. The medicine man and locals claim that he cursed the land upon his demise. They say that he still roams the grounds of the cemetery in search of new victims and souls he can barter for a return to his living days.

This cursed land is said to have played out on generations of the Gilson family, who built the stone walls and placed a small farmhouse on it. The original home burned to the ground, with several family members perishing inside. They were buried on the property, and the home was rebuilt. Several years later, the new home met the same fate as the first, with further Gilson family members also dying. No future homes were raised on the site, but more and more Gilsons (as well as other local families) were buried in the rural cemetery.

John Gilson, likely the namesake of the cemetery, has a stone beside three smaller stones labeled simply "Baby Gilson." During the time period of the deaths, it was quite common that children and infants met early deaths, and it appears that the Gilson family had many members who also did not make it to their adulthoods. Given the poor condition of many of the stones in the grounds, resulting from time, weather, and vandals, some believe that it is the spirit of John Gilson who tries to dissuade visitors from coming too close to his family's remains.

AUTHOR'S NOTE

I visited Gilson Cemetery with my fellow paranormal investigator Cathy McManus (Cat). Though it was a bright and sunny fall day on a well-traveled road, there was something about the cemetery that just felt "off." It wasn't the poor state of many of the stones, or anything else that may make it appear "creepy" per se, but I noticed instantly after exiting the car a foreboding air to the location.

I have investigated many haunted locations over the years and frankly would have relished having an experience to report, but I had never experienced a feeling of such desire to leave a location. While we all have a "fight or flight" instinct, this location really set off my bells and whistles. While Cat entered the cemetery gates to take some close-up shots of the damaged stones in the cemetery, I elected to stay outside the stone wall bordering the road to take distance shots of the grounds and gate. It was a very intense sensation that we were intruding where we were most definitely not welcome.

Though Cat also described the vibe of the setting as "oppressive," she did not necessarily have any difficulties entering the grounds, so after approximately fifteen minutes, I elected to push aside my gut instincts and join her inside. With a deep breath, I took off walking along the wall toward the gate. Though I briefly questioned what sounded like heavy footsteps following close behind, I pushed on through the gates—and instantly regretted this choice. Less than three feet in from the gate I was hit with a blinding migraine complete with visual disturbances and strong nausea.

I quickly returned to the car while Cat rapidly completed taking photos. Though I had driven us there in my vehicle, I had been rendered unable to drive. I handed the keys to Cat, and she drove us away in search of some Advil. I attempted not to get ill in the car, though this turned out to be an unfounded fear. Rather, when we were less than a mile from the cemetery, the migraine suddenly and completely vanished. I had not to that date, and not since, been so significantly affected in a paranormally charged locale. It served as an important reminder of the need to pay attention to warnings my body may be giving me, and I encourage you to always do the same. —S. P.

Gilson Cemetery.

DIRECTIONS

Gilson Cemetery is located on Gilson Road, across from Tanglewood Drive, in Nashua, New Hampshire. Though the cemetery is on city-owned land, it is entered by foot only, and there is no designated parking. Please try to park safely away from the rock wall, preferably on the cemetery side of the road and not in front of the private residences across the street. Due to some vandalism complaints and damages to tombstones, a sign was erected stating, "purposeful damage to this property may be punishable by seven years of imprisonment and a $10,000 fine," and the location is patrolled by the Nashua Police Department, so please take extra care when visiting.

ALSO NEARBY

The County Tavern Restaurant and Pub at 452 Amherst Street is a restored 1741 farmhouse with a bit of a dark history. The farm is reportedly haunted by a ghost named Elizabeth, who was murdered at the site by her seafaring husband when he returned from a voyage of over a year to discover that she had recently given birth. In a fit of rage at her betrayal, he murdered both her and the child, throwing her down the well before burying the baby under a tree. Local lore states that she never left the property, and you can visit with her restless soul while enjoying a locally brewed beer and ordering some "Chicken Elizabeth" in her honor. Visit www.countrytavern.org for more information.

Blood Cemetery

HOLLIS, NEW HAMPSHIRE

SITE HISTORY

Nestled in the woods of Hollis, New Hampshire, is a small plot of land considered by many to be one of the most haunted spots in all of New England. Frequently topping the lists of ghostly destinations that flood the Internet each fall, Pine Hill Cemetery has earned a strong reputation with paranormal enthusiasts. Electronic voice phenomena, ghostly orbs, camera malfunctions, EMF spikes, and even car radios spontaneously playing funeral dirge music as they drive past the property all have been reported. Though it is widely known by locals as "Blood Cemetery," it is not for any of these spooky reasons, however. Rather, the cemetery has been given the eponymous nickname from the many members of the Blood family who are interred there.

In 1769, local farmer Benjamin Parker Jr. donated the peaceful hilltop area to the town of Hollis. The town immediately made use of the spot to lay to rest their Christians, and more than 300 people were buried here before it reached capacity. Many of these stones were for Revolutionary War veterans and are older than the earliest incorporation dates of many US states. As a result of advanced age, the majority of these stones have become badly weathered and damaged and have been subsequently removed, resulting in numerous unmarked graves.

Top: Pine Hill Cemetery, a.k.a. "Blood Cemetery."
Below: Blood family plot, with Abel Blood's broken stone on the far right.

One of these unmarked graves belongs to Abel Blood. Buried in the cemetery in 1867, just seventeen years after California joined the Union, his stone quickly gave rise to an urban legend shortly after his interment. His stone featured a finger facing heavenward, as was a popular style in its day, that reportedly would morph and point hellward by night. He was rumored to have been murdered in a family massacre at a nearby farmhouse, and Abel is said to roam the cemetery grounds searching for his fellow fallen family members. Modern visitors to the cemetery are also left searching, since vandals broke the stone and threw it into nearby Gilson Cemetery, and it was never repaired and replaced.

The tortured soul of a young Blood family boy has also been seen trying to flag down cars on the dark and hilly road outside the cemetery. He begs for help but disappears if you stop your vehicle and try to approach him.

OUR VISIT

We visited the cemetery on a mild, late-spring afternoon. Though the weather was warm, we were unprepared for the temperature increase that greeted us as we entered the wide-openness of the center of the cemetery grounds. Quick digital temperature readings recorded an increase of over ten degrees in temperature and a nearly fifteen percent increase in relative humidity from the center of the cemetery as compared to the area just outside it. The sun beat down on us as we made our way around the grounds. Due to the many missing stones and the resulting unmarked graves, we both commented on feeling the unsettled sensation of inadvertently disrespecting the dead by walking upon the unmarked remains.

While investigating the grounds, we were drawn to the right rear corner by the Farley family plot and were able to receive a few Ghost Box responses to our questions that appeared intelligent in nature. Our video camera batteries depleted in just a few moments despite being brand new, and our digital still camera malfunctioned several times, having difficulties focusing and twice failing to properly save images on the camera card. We were also struck by how quiet it was within the cemetery, despite being along a frequently traveled road. Since there are trees on all sides of the grounds, and we were there alone, it was easy to see how sounds could travel, and multiple times we heard shuffling footsteps and throat-clearing noises around us. It was difficult to determine where these noises had come from, and it was easy to see that this phenomenon would be particularly unnerving by nightfall.

Both of us also remarked that we felt watched, but again, we found a likely cause for this. Motion-activated cameras with floodlights were mounted in all four corners of the property and likely took hundreds of images of us as we moved about among the stones. Due to the vandalism that has occurred, the cemetery is now regularly patrolled, especially around Halloween, and though visitors are welcome to the grounds by day, those who cause damage or trespass at night will likely be prosecuted.

DIRECTIONS

Pine Hill / Blood Cemetery is located on Nartoff Road in Hollis, New Hampshire. Though there is no official street number for the cemetery grounds, it is near Lavoie's Farm at 172 Nartoff Road. There is space for parking one or two cars just outside the grounds or along the roadside.

Stephen King

BANGOR, MAINE

18

SITE HISTORY

Portland-born Stephen Edwin King is arguably Maine's most famous resident. The author of contemporary horror, supernatural fiction, suspense, and fantasy books, many of which are set in Maine, he has published fifty-four-plus novels, including seven under the pen name of Richard Bachman, six nonfiction works, and over 200 short stories, selling over 350 million copies worldwide at the time of this writing. A great number of his works have been adapted into successful feature films, miniseries, TV shows, and comic books.

This international publishing has afforded King and his wife, Tabitha, the luxury of owning and occupying three homes. In addition to wintering in Sarasota, Florida, the Kings have homes in Lovell and Bangor, Maine. It is the home in a quiet neighborhood just outside downtown Bangor that draws thousands of visitors annually to the area. The large red-and-white home is much like the others on West Broadway Street, but it is the fence and gate that hints at the owner's darker side. Fans by the droves stop to admire the black wrought-iron spider's webs, bat-winged creatures, and a three-headed reptilian monster.

Just a short distance away, you can visit the settings and filming locations central to some of King's most favorite novels and films. The largest of these sites is the Thomas Hill Standpipe on Thomas Hill Road. This real-life water supplier for the city of

Stephen King's home in Bangor, Maine.

Bangor served as the inspiration for the haunted water tower in 1986's *It*. In addition to an outstanding view, if you take one of the available guided tours, you can visit the small park where King reportedly wrote most of the novel on a small park bench.

Though different in style from the film version, the storm drain that inspired the scene where Pennywise the Clown pulled in little Geordie Denbrough sits at the corner of Jackson and Union Streets.

Fans of *Pet Sematary* may spot the cemetery location where the Bragg family patriarch disinterred his young son beside a distinctively steep stone staircase, and where Stephen King cameoed as a reverend conducting a funeral is easily spotted at nearby Mount Hope Cemetery. The distinctive red-roofed yellow farmhouse, which iconically served as the Bragg family home, is approximately one hour away in the small town of Hancock, Maine.

AUTHOR'S NOTE

Though the Kings welcome fans to take pictures of their home and often will stop for photos with you and their dog, Molly, "the Thing of Evil," please be extra vigilant about not trespassing or infringing on their personal space or that of their neighbors. Several notable incidences of violations of these boundaries have occurred, including a man stalking Tabitha and breaking into the home, bomb threats, and even a mentally disturbed man handing out "evidence" that King killed John Lennon—and the police do regularly patrol. As always, appreciate the sites and visit the Kings in a manner that allows the continued viewing of the house without any large trees or hedges being planted to block the way.

Filming site of Pet Sematary.

Thomas Hill Standpipe.

DIRECTIONS

Stephen King's house is located at 47 West Broadway Street in Bangor, Maine.

The Standpipe inspiration is on Thomas Hill Road in Bangor, Maine

Pet Sematary filming sites: Mount Hope Cemetery. Enter at the gate at 1048 State Street in Bangor, Maine. Take the first road to the right after entering the cemetery grounds, and you will spot the stone steps to the left of the road. The filming site for the Bragg family home is located at 303 Point Road in Hancock, Maine.

USS *Maine* Memorial

BANGOR, MAINE

SITE HISTORY

Remember the Maine!

—Slogan of the Spanish-American War

In 1898, an armored US Navy cruiser was sent to Cuba as merely a precautionary measure to ensure the safety of Americans during the Cuban War of Independence. On February 15, 1898, a still highly debated explosion erupted, causing the ship to rapidly sink, killing three-quarters of the crew, 260 men in all. Despite protests of innocence by Spain (Cuba's colonial seat of power), Americans remained convinced of their guilt, and tensions between the countries persisted, directly leading to the Spanish-American War.

In 1912, the shield and scrolls from the doomed ship were able to be recovered from the harbor floor, and in 1922 the city of Bangor commissioned local architect Edwin S. Kent to create a permanent memorial in Davenport Park. Fastened to a twelve-foot-tall, life-sized granite plinth, the memorial is meant to represent a ship's bow.

The USS *Maine* Memorial in Bangor, Maine.

DIRECTIONS

Prominently displayed at 35 Cedar Street, across from the Bangor Police Department, the park is peaceful despite its downtown location. It is easily accessible, with ample parking in a lot immediately beside the memorial.

ALSO VISIT

Additional memorials to the USS *Maine* include a cannon at Fort Allen Park on the Eastern Promenade in Portland, Maine, and a recovered projectile at Veterans Memorial Park at the corner of Main and Lincoln Streets in Lewiston.

Korean War Memorial

BANGOR, MAINE

SITE HISTORY

I walked among my comrades brave,
upon that bloody hill
And saw no movement, none at all,
for it was deathly still.
There were no cries from trembling lips,
no soldier's blasphemy;
I called their names out, every one,
but no one answered me.

I know each rock, each clump of trees
that marks this hallowed ground
For in my mind I see them fall
and I hear that battle sound.
Now the silence takes my breath
for all that I can see
Are rows on rows of crosses
where old comrades used to be.

"Old Comrades" by Thomas Lynn

Korean War Memorial in Mount Hope Cemetery, Bangor, Maine.

In 1992, a group of motivated veterans recognized the need to memorialize all Maine service men and women, but especially the 245 Maine men who were killed during the Korean War. After three years of fundraising, encompassing everything from bake sales to car raffles, and many challenges related to what the most appropriate location for the memorial would be, Mount Hope Cemetery in Bangor, Maine, was selected.

MAINE

Sitting beside a small pond, the Korean War Memorial features a pagoda-styled crosspiece that sits on top of granite slabs engraved with the names of the 245 Mainers lost. As you approach this testament to the Forgotten War, you see the national flag, flanked on either side by the state of Maine and United Nations flags. The UN flags are displayed in order of battle losses, beginning with the Republic of Korea and ending with Turkey. Just below these are flags honoring the five American military services' logos. A Victor's Walkway is engraved with eulogy stones for veterans, leading to a plaque containing the poem "Old Comrades," written by Korean War veteran Thomas Lynn.

Civil War memorial.

DIRECTIONS

The Korean War Memorial is located at Mount Hope Cemetery in Bangor, Maine. Mount Hope Cemetery was the second garden-style cemetery, opening in 1836, and was inspired by the Mount Auburn Cemetery in Cambridge, Massachusetts. On its 264 acres you will find a large tract of land with ponds, bowers, grottoes, and a variety of plantings and wildlife. An online map at their website (www.mthopebgr.com), with searchable interment list, can help you find your way to any of the over 30,000 final resting places.

Though the main gates are located at 1048 State Street, the Korean War Memorial is most easily accessed through the gate at Eastern Street, from where it is prominently visible. There is parking within the interior cemetery roads, and the location is handicapped accessible. The memorial is illuminated May through November, with special observances held on Memorial Day, June 25, July 27, United Nations Day, Flag Day, and Veterans Day. The cemetery itself is open daily from dawn to dusk.

ALSO NEARBY

Just behind the Korean War Memorial you will see a small bridge leading to a castle-styled Civil War memorial that is also worth visiting.

Grave of Vice President Hannibal Hamlin

BANGOR, MAINE

SITE HISTORY

Born August 27, 1809, Hannibal Hamlin died on the 4th of July 1891, while playing cards at the Tarratine Club in Bangor. Hamlin served as the fifteenth vice president of the United States under President Abraham Lincoln during the first three years of the Civil War. When Lincoln ran for his second term, Hamlin was passed over in favor of Andrew Johnson. Over the course of his political career, Hamlin also served as a senator, congressman, and minister to Spain.

The Hamlin family plot.

DIRECTIONS

Enter Mount Hope Cemetery in Bangor, Maine, through the State Street entrance. As you enter, take note of the impressive Civil War Memorial and its ornate angel relief.

Take the first road to the right, on the road that runs parallel to State Street. Along this road you will also find several *Pet Sematary* filming locations. (See page 47.)

ALSO NEARBY

Dysart's Truck Stop at 530 Cold Brook Road in Hermon, Maine, offers hearty fare, including burgers, pasta, steaks, and more. Popular with truckers, locals, and visitors to the area, this local gem is a must-stop when you are in the area. Open twenty-four hours a day, swing in for some fantastic comfort food. A personal favorite of mine is the bacon cheeseburger mac and cheese, while my son is a fan of getting free seconds on crinkle fries and home fries. View their extensive menu at www.dysarts.com.

MAINE

Buck's Memorial

BUCKSPORT, MAINE

Detail of the headstone anomaly at Buck's Memorial.

SITE HISTORY

Colonel Jonathan Buck, the founder and namesake of the city of Bucksport, Maine, was a regional Revolutionary War hero. It is not his military prowess that placed his name among notable Mainers, however. Rather, it was his tombstone that has made the Buck name the stuff of legend.

When Buck passed away in 1795, he was buried in the small family plot in the eastern part of the town. In 1852, his grandchildren erected a large monument to him toward the front of the plot, and as it weathered, an image of a woman's leg and foot and a sideways heart appeared above the Buck name. Stories instantly started being passed around town when they materialized, but they really began to spread when the story was covered in the *Haverhill Gazette* in 1899. It was their telling of the tale that quickly began spreading as the "official" one.

The *Gazette* reported that Colonel Buck was a Puritan with a hatred of anything impure and un-Godlike. When a local woman was accused of witchcraft, he fought to see her sentenced to execution by being burned at the stake. The *Haverhill Gazette* stated, "the hangman was about to perform the gruesome duty when the woman turned to Colonel Buck and raising one hand to heaven, as if to direct her last words on earth, and pronounced this astounding prophecy:

Jonathan Buck, listen to these words, the last my tongue will utter. It is the spirit of the only true and loving God, which bids me speak them to you. You will soon die. Over your grave they will erect a stone that all may know where your bones are crumbling into dust. But listen, upon that stone the imprint of my feet will appear, and for all time, long after you and your accursed race have perished from the earth, will the people from far and wide know that you murdered a woman. Remember well, Jonathan Buck, remember well.

The story has been retold in different variations in the intervening 117 years. Two popular variations include the name of the woman being Sarah Williams and a lover of Col. Buck, whom he accused of witchcraft when she became pregnant and he wanted to avoid any scandalous damage to his reputation. In a more gruesome telling, during the woman's execution, her leg and foot became dislodged and rolled out of the fire, which was then grabbed by "her deformed son," who further cursed Buck before running away with the limb into the woods, never to be seen again.

Historical research casts some significant doubts on the urban legends. First, the timeline does not correlate with the witchcraft hysteria occurring in the region (Buck was born more than twenty-five years after the trials in Salem), and no record exists of any witchcraft executions occurring in Maine. Further, Col. Buck was a justice of the peace and would have had no authority to condemn anyone to death. None of these facts have diminished the strength of the legend; attempts that have been made to remove the image have been unsuccessful, and the leg and foot always return. Some professionals experienced with monuments suggest it is a natural flaw in the stone, perhaps a vein of iron, which darkens through contact with oxygen. Regardless of the cause, the image and the legend live on.

DIRECTIONS

Buck Monument is located at Buck Cemetery on Main Street in Bucksport, Maine. It is directly across from the Hanneford Supermarket, and the monument is easily spotted. There is a small parking area and a ramp that allows handicapped accessibility. Though a locked gate and fence keeps visitors from entering the actual cemetery grounds, the ramp takes you right beside the monument, where a sign and a plaque tell the tale.

23

Fort Knox

PROSPECT, MAINE

SITE HISTORY

During the Revolutionary War and the War of 1812, the Penobscot River in Maine saw British ships by the score sail up its length. During both wars, Great Britain took control over the river, fought battles in the river valley towns, and claimed the land for the British Empire. Though the British claims to the area did not last, the United States Government was convinced of the need to establish a center of defense along the river to keep it from becoming susceptible to losses in the rapidly growing towns nearby, including the state capitol of Bangor.

In May 1844, land was acquired in Prospect, Maine, and the US Department of War Corps of Engineers began building Fort Knox, named after Major General Henry Knox, America's first secretary of war and commander of artillery during the American Revolution. Coincidentally, the other "Fort Knox," in Kentucky, was named after the same man.

The fort was built with four batteries (A–D), two levels, and mounts for up to 135 cannons. The large central fort building contained men's quarters, powder magazines, parade grounds, and even a bakery. The fort was used for two periods of military activity. During the Civil War, twenty to fifty-four troops were stationed at the fort, and about 575 troops from Connecticut lived at the fort during the Spanish-American War. Though enemy ships were never spotted during either war, the fort did give substantial peace of mind to the area's towns.

Fort Knox in Prospect, Maine.

Fort Knox exterior.

source present. Stories are told of the spirits of a little girl named Elizabeth and a man named Mike, both of whom are capable of physical interaction and object manipulation and have interacted with dozens of paranormal investigation teams; the experiences of the East Coast Ghost Trackers, who call the fort their home base, contributed to the 2013 book *The Haunted Fort* by Liza Gardner Walsh, which details the spookier happenings on the location.

Today, the grounds and buildings are maintained by the "Friends of the Fort Knox." You can wander freely through the dark hallways and rooms. Several times a year, especially during the summer months, costumed reenactors help visitors discover the history of the fort. The "Fright at the Fort" events held annually in October are particularly popular.

Though the fort never saw any fighting, and no one is known to have died there, it has earned a reputation of being one of Maine's most haunted locations. The popular SyFy channel show *Ghost Hunters* filmed the seventh episode of their seventh season there, where they verified the claims and experienced thermal-imaging anomalies, laser grid disturbances, and loud unexplained breathing in Long Alley; footsteps and a red-light anomaly in the casemates; and K-2 (a form of EMF meter used by paranormal investigators) disturbances in the officer's quarters, where there is no electrical

AUTHOR'S NOTE

I visited Fort Knox on a sunny summer afternoon but found there were plenty of chills to be had in the fort. Not only is the temperature significantly cooler once inside the buildings, it is easy to see why people get creeped out at the spot. We constantly felt watched and expected phantom hands to reach out and grab at us from the many dark doorways. At times we heard footsteps directly behind us, though we were alone in the casemates at the time. There were areas that I could not convince my nine-year-old son to enter (despite having withheld the ghost stories from him, and his being ordinarily quite daring). I wouldn't doubt that there are many spirits that call the fort home. —S .P.

DIRECTIONS

Fort Knox Historic Site is located at 740 Fort Knox Road in Prospect, Maine. The site is open May–October from 9:00 a.m. to sunset. Visit http://maine.gov/mdot/pnbo/fortknox/ for information on special events.

ALSO NEARBY

Also on the site is the Penobscot Narrows Bridge and Observatory. The viewing area at the top is at 420 feet and is forty-two stories high, making it taller than the Statue of Liberty. From the top you can see an excellent 360-degree view of Fort Knox, the city of Bucksport, and the Maine countryside. It is the only observatory bridge in the Western Hemisphere, and the tallest one of its kind in the world.

24

The Witch's Grave

BOWDOIN, MAINE

SITE HISTORY

Lizzie Lydstrom
Sept. 16, 1869
To My Earth Friends,
This is to tell you I still live.
In mansions in the spirit world,
There is no death, this truth believe.
O 'tis a greater wealth than gold.
Nor have I gone far-off—above—
my heaven home's with those I love.
'Tis Lizzie's thought in Spirit Sphere.
These words impressed as written here.

Yours affectionately, in Spirit,
Love and Live, Lizzie

Had local authors Charlene B. Bartlett and Jayne E. Bickford not thought to make a rubbing of Lizzie's stone while researching their book *Cemetery Inscriptions and Revolutionary, War of 1812 and Civil War Veterans of Bowdoin, Maine*, the true story of Lizzie's stone would likely have been lost to history. Just weeks after they made note of the stone, an unknown party also made note of its novelty, and it was stolen from North Cemetery, never to be recovered.

The Witch's Grave in Bowdoin, Maine.

As is often the case with historical information, in absence of hard facts, urban legends spring up to fill in the gaps. If you ask the locals of Bowdoin about the legend surrounding Lizzie's grave, off to the side of the cemetery, they will readily tell you that she was a witch. Accused, tried, and hanged in the town square, due to the nature of her "crime" they elected to bury her, but not in the small cemetery on Litchfield Road. Surrounded by a ring of cedar trees that are not present in the surrounding woods sat the solitary stone. A nearby tree stump was rumored to display a star when Lizzie's restless spirit was roaming the pit seeking her vengeance. A curse awaits any and all who are foolish enough to enter the ring of trees, and are forever cursed to a life of woe.

The center of the plot is sunken in, without any notable vegetation growing on it, with only the small stone base where the unique tombstones once sat. How this depression occurred is contested but may result from the decomposition of the nearly 150-year-old wooden coffin, causing soil displacement above it. Local legend is that three teenagers were unsuccessfully attempting to disinter Lizzie and were all killed in tragic accidents that very week. Either way, the way that the site presents itself has been enough to keep Lizzie's name on the lips of Maine young people since 1869.

AUTHOR'S NOTE

While visiting the cemetery, I was struck by its poor condition. Very few of the stones were undamaged. It would seem that the area is irregularly maintained and even less often visited, and it appears to have fallen victim to vandalism, such as the hole in this monument, which appears unlikely to have been caused by natural forces. Though it is no longer permitted to take rubbings of graveyard stones due to the damage that it causes them, Bartlett and Bickford's rubbing is all that remains to give clues to who Lizzie Lydstrom really was in life. This is why we try to take as many photographs as possible when we visit a site. There is no way of knowing how or when these vital records can be destroyed. Visit sites such as North Cemetery with the attitude of a historian and preservationist.

Though calm and quiet at North Cemetery, save for the occasional car driving by, as my son and I walked the grounds taking photographs and commenting on the stones, we very much did not feel alone. We both frequently caught movement out of the corner of our eyes, and the sensation of feeling watched was ever present. Though we did not see a star on the tree stump, we did not feel compelled to enter the ring of trees. Whether you believe in the curse or not, with Lizzie's grave being unmarked due to theft, I didn't feel the desire to further disrupt her eternal rest. We found it more advantageous to follow her advice to "love and live" and leave her in peace. —S. P.

North Cemetery in Bowdoin, Maine.

DIRECTIONS

North Cemetery is located on Litchfield Road, just past Dead River Road when heading west. No parking area is present, so park safely along the road. Due to the uneven terrain, it may not be suitable for visitation to those with mobility issues, regardless of age.

MAINE

25

The Pirates of Northern New England

PENOBSCOT AND CASCO BAYS, MAINE

Penobscot Bay, as seen from Monhegan Island.

SITE HISTORY

Now and then we had a hope that if we lived and were good, God would permit us to be pirates.

—Mark Twain, *Life on the Mississippi*

When we think of pirates, most of us think of the romanticized rogues hailing from England or Spain, sailing over aqua-blue seas and swashbuckling around the Caribbean. In actuality, pirates have been around since the dawn of travel and commerce along the waterway trade routes of the world and began out of necessity.

Living as a pirate was extremely difficult and unhealthful and usually meant meeting a perilous end. Early pirates originated in European places such as Greece, Spain, and England, and even more northern territories such as Norway. They eventually followed the trade to the New World of the Americas and then gathered new shipmates and captains out of the New England colonies. For approximately seventy-five years, beginning in the mid-seventeenth century, pirates were a real and notorious presence along the coast of New England, which, during this golden age of piracy, was nicknamed the "Gold Coast."

With the implementation of the Navigation Acts of the 1690s, in which the government of England decided to oppress and restrict the use of foreign ships in trade, the need for "privateering" emerged as merchants sought out alternative incomes. These privateers initially set sail, employed by local merchants, but they quickly decided to go out on their own as plunderers of treasure for their own quick profits. These seamen found their way to popular and emerging seaports around the world, which included the New England coast.

In most of these ports, pirates were generally accepted and welcomed as a common part of trade activity. The privateers were there to trade and restocked their ships with important supplies including food, gunpowder, and alcohol, finding respite from their boat quarters in local inns. Of course, some also sought out safe havens if they were wanted for crimes. It is a fact that many New Englanders were recruited or even forced into becoming pirates when the need for additional shipmates arose. After all, pirates were in the business of obtaining riches and power over the seas and needed lots of manpower to do so. It was through these fierce interactions that they earned their lasting historical reputations.

Included were the stories of notorious buccaneers such as Captain William Kidd, Edward "Blackbeard" Teach, "Black Sam" Samuel Bellamy, and Jack Quelch, just to name a few who roamed the waters off Boston's North Shore while so-called witches were being hanged at Salem.

DIXIE BULL

Dixie Bull was active in piracy for just a short period, sailing the coast of Maine from 1631 to 1633. He is credited with being the first documented pirate to emerge from the New England area. His birth, actual name, and exact date of death are not precisely known. He was an independent English privateer working largely alone in the Indian trade around the Penobscot Bay area when he shamelessly attacked the "defended" settlement of Pemaquid. This behavior was not the norm for sailing traders of that day and earned him the name "the Dread Pirate." His vessel was then overtaken and plundered by a group of roving French pirates. In retaliation, he traveled back to Boston and convinced a group of approximately twenty men to assist in recouping his losses after his complaint in a Boston court did not yield a satisfactory response. His disappearance from the Maine coast is based on hearsay and legend, since there are no official records to be found.

As with many pirate tales, there are some poems and ballads in ode to Dixie Bull. Some say he died in battle on the coast of Maine, and others say that he was hanged upon arriving back in his native England. There are also legends that say he may have buried his booty on any number of islands that he had visited in Penobscot Bay off Boothbay Harbor, or in Casco Bay off the Port of Portland, Maine. Treasure has yet to be found.

NED LOW

Edward "Ned" Low was a self-made and especially brutal pirate hailing from Boston. A particularly nasty character, his Jolly Roger flag depicted a blood-red skeleton. He had a fleet of about three to four ships and is known for capturing at least one hundred ships and inflicting horrific torture and cruelties upon its crews and captains. One such capture is the Spanish galleon the *Montcova*, where it is said that he himself killed fifty-three officers and made one of the men cut out and eat the heart of his shipmate before being killed himself.

Ned Low terrorized the seas for a relatively short three years, and his ending is greatly speculated. There does not seem to be a clear documentation of his actual death, only that reports of his activities had halted over a period of time, and it was assumed that he had met his ultimate fate. The most popular rumor of his demise was that he had been set out to sea in a dingy with no food or provisions and left to the cruelties of the open ocean by his own crew, and that a passing French ship had found and rescued him but made him "walk the plank" upon discovering his identity.

There is still treasure-hunter activity around Low's old haunts, such as Isles of Shoals off the coasts of Maine and New Hampshire and Nova Scotia's Isle Haute in the Bay of Fundy, by those searching for artifacts of ships that he sank.

PHILIP ASHTON

Philip Ashton was born in Marblehead, Massachusetts, and he told a tale that in the year 1722, at the age of nineteen years, he was forcibly recruited by Edward "Ned" Low as he was fishing alone along the coast of Nova Scotia. It is documented that Philip was uncooperative and refused to sign the captain's articles of agreement and was therefore chained, beaten, and kept onboard as a captive throughout Captain Low's travels. Ashton's memoirs were published in 1725, in Boston, as an article titled "History of the Strange Adventures and Signal Deliverances of Mr. Philip Ashton." The account detailed his escape from Captain Low's ship by hiding out in the jungles of Roatan, an island off the coast of Honduras, as Low's ship departed. He chronicled learning to survive on what seafood he could capture, native fruit he could pluck, and what jungle cover he could find for sixteen months before being rescued by a passing ship out of Salem, Massachusetts.

BLACKBEARD (EDWARD TEACH)

Although Ocracoke Inlet in North Carolina was his base of operations, Blackbeard terrorized the New England coast. Teach's beard was the talk of two continents. Jet black, his beard completely covered his face, even growing around his eyes and giving him a fierce appearance. He never took marriage seriously, and during his lifetime he had fourteen wives and fathered forty children. In 1691, he and a sizeable crew landed at Lunging Island in the Isles of Shoals off Portsmouth, New Hampshire. There, it is said, he buried a large treasure of silver bars that has never been discovered.

CAPTAIN KIDD

William Kidd, also known as Captain Kidd, was another one of America's most famous romanticized pirates. Although much of William Kidd's family background is either disputed or not verifiable, it is agreed that he was born in Scotland, and most accounts describe his father as a seaman who was most likely lost at sea.

Similar to many pirates, William Kidd became familiar with the sea at a young age and began a seaward life as a privateer. William was a wealthy man by marriage and was hired by Lord Bellomont, Royal Governor of Massachusetts, to seek out and capture Blackbeard. Failing to capture him, Kidd became a pirate himself—although he denied being one until his dying day. Returning to Boston in 1699, Kidd was arrested and shipped to London for trial. He was sentenced to be hanged at Execution Dock in London on May 23, 1701. On the first attempt the rope broke, but the sheriff's men dragged him back to the gallows and hanged him successfully the second time. Kidd's body was painted with tar, wrapped in chains, and placed in an iron cage on the riverbank. For almost twenty years, his body remained gibbeted as an example to other would-be pirates.

He left behind an urban legend that has inspired treasure hunters for hundreds of years. Kidd was rumored to have come to Monhegan Island and hidden a chest of treasure in a cave with an opening to the sea, protected by the watchful eye of powerful spirits. Searchers once found the cave and the heavy trunk within and were about to take it away when one of them spoke—against explicit orders. The spell was broken and the guarding spirits took notice and snatched back the treasure. Some years later, the cave was blasted to enlarge it in hopes of finding the chest after it became a frequently told tale. It was often said, "Dig six feet and you will find iron; dig six more and you will find money."

"BLACK SAM" BELLAMY

"Black Sam" Bellamy, also known as the "Prince of Pirates" or the "Romantic Pirate," is credited with being the wealthiest pirate in recorded history. Before the age of twenty-eight, and with his heaviest activity in piracy lasting approximately one year, he had in excess of fifty ships under his capture and amassed a total fortune that in today's world would be valued at approximately 131 million dollars.

What is known about Samuel Bellamy's early years is that he was born in Devonshire, England, and became interested in sailing at a young age when his family moved to the busy port of Plymouth, England. He joined the Royal Navy as a teen and then decided to wander off toward the coast of Cape Cod, Massachusetts, and Rhode Island to meet up with relatives.

There is some local folklore told in the Cape that Sam took up a romantic relationship with Goody (Maria) Hallet, a woman who came to be known after the fact as the "Witch of Wellfleet" or the "Billingsgate Witch." The historical record of her exact demographics or the full nature of their relationship is not clear, although there are many romantic and speculative theories on it. The main theme though is that Sam wished to win Ms. Hallet's hand and knew that her Christian Catholic family did not approve of his current standing. Legend has it that Sam vowed to find a fortune and return to her on the Cape.

A determined Bellamy then left Cape Cod for the coastal waters of Florida after hearing of a Spanish wreck with great treasures aboard. When that expedition had unsuccessful results, he joined a pirate crew on the ship *Marianne*, whose first mate, Edward Teach (a.k.a. "Blackbeard"), was still relatively unknown. Within a year, this crew elected Bellamy as commander and captain of the *Marianne*. Captain Bellamy and his crew looted some fifty Spanish and English galleons and then came upon the fairly new English galley the *Whydah* (*Ouida*), which was a slave ship on sail to home from Jamaica with a large cargo of goods, including silver and gold. The captain and crew of the *Whydah* eluded Bellamy for three days before he overtook it "without a fight." Bellamy then made the prized *Whydah* his flagship and proceeded to sail northward. As fate would have it, Sam never made it back to his beloved Maria Hallet. In April 1717, off Cape Cod just before reaching Wellfleet (said to be only 1,640 feet or 500 meters), the *Whydah* ran into an especially nasty and powerful nor'easter. The storm battered the great ship and pushed it onto the shoals of Cape Cod, where it was smashed to pieces, killing Bellamy and all but two of his men. Oddly enough, most seamen of the time could not swim!

Be assured, the two survivors, Thomas Davis and John Julian, were rounded up and brought to trial for piracy. Thomas Davis was acquitted because he was found to have been forced against his will (used onboard for his carpentry skills), and John Julian, who was a dark-skinned Central American and skilled navigator, was reportedly sold into slavery to none other than Colonel John Quincy, the namesake of the city of Quincy, Massachusetts, and maternal grandfather of the sixth president of the United States, John Quincy Adams.

The wreck of the *Whydah* rested at the bottom of this "Graveyard of the Atlantic" not to be detected until 1982, when archaeological ocean explorer Barry Clifford discovered pieces of the wreck in just sixteen feet of water and ten feet of sand. The *Whydah* Pirate Museum in Yarmouth, Massachusetts, and the original Expedition *Whydah* in Provincetown, Massachusetts, can be toured to learn more. Items found include the ship's engraved bell, the anchor, clothing, and the most treasure ever discovered by any expedition. In addition, a Bellamy legend was confirmed when Clifford's group found an eleven-inch human fibula bone encased in a silk stocking protruding out of a size five leather shoe.

Upon scientific testing, it was found to belong to a child of no older than eleven years. It had been long told that a young boy named James King, who had not yet reached the age of ten, had voluntarily joined the Bellamy crew after the ship he was traveling on with his family was commandeered. On this account, James King is the youngest known pirate on record. Suffice to say the story of "Black Sam" Bellamy and his flagship *Whydah* is one of the most amazing, fascinating, and truly authentic in New England pirate lore.

OUR VISIT

We are blessed to live in Maine and have visited many of the small islands in Casco and Penobscot Bays that were frequented by pirates, including Monhegan Island, located twelve miles off the coastline. In addition to potentially being home to Captain Kidd's cave-bound treasure, the island was visited on April 29, 1717, by the pirate ship *Anne*. The ship, led by Captain Bonita, had been captured off the Virginia Capes by Samuel Bellamy and the *Whydah*, and they waited to rendezvous with the ship there. After they became aware that the ship had wrecked off Cape Cod, the crew of the *Anne* eventually discovered that the *Whydah* had been lost, and they proceeded to attack vessels at Matinicus and Pemaquid Islands. Today, the island is a wonderful diversion from city life, and the town of seventy-five has a vibrant and thriving arts community. —S. P.

DIRECTIONS

Casco Bay Lines out of Portland, Maine, holds regularly scheduled scenic, music, and special-event cruises. The Mailboat Run is particularly popular and is a true working boat delivering mail and packages to Little Diamond, Great Diamond, Long Cliff, and Chebeaque Islands. These cruises run year-round, and schedules can be viewed at www.cascobaylines.com .

Penobscot Bay and its many lighthouses can be viewed by chartering trips through Matinicus Excursions by calling 207-691-9030 or emailing gtarkleson@yahoo.com.

The Maine State Ferry Service also runs a ferry from Lincolnville to Uslebor to see the Grindle Point Lighthouse, and from Rockland to Browns Head Light, Heron Neck Lighthouse, and Goose Rocks Lighthouse. Call 1-800-491-4883 for more information.

To visit Monhegan Island, you can travel from Port Clyde, New Harbor, and Boothbay Harbor. Visit www.monheganwelcome.com or the Monhegan Boat Line at www.monheganboat.com.

MAINE

Anderson-Smith Cemetery

SOUTH WINDHAM, MAINE

26

SITE HISTORY

This cemetery, sometimes referred to as "Old Smith" or "Old Anderson" burying ground, is located in South Windham, Maine. It is the only burial ground for the original parsonage in this area and holds members of the Anderson and Smith families (related by marriage) as well as the original parishioners of Parson Smith's congregation. The Parson Smith House and the Anderson-Smith Cemetery were built in 1764 by Peter Thatcher Smith, the son of Reverend or "Parson" Smith, who had relocated from Portland and founded this first Congregational ministry. The home remains virtually unaltered from that time and is listed on the National Register of Historic Places, and although it was once run as a museum, it is currently a private home. The homestead overlooks the family and parsonage cemetery known as Anderson-Smith Cemetery. The history, lineage, and papers of the Anderson and Smith families are well documented and preserved as the Parson Smith Family Papers, a seven-section collection of family and local-area documents managed through the Historic New England Heritage organization.

Side view of the Anderson family crypt.

The Den at Anderson-Smith Cemetery in Windham, Maine.

There is local folklore told about ghostly activity around these two interest points, as well as in the parking area of this cemetery.

OUR VISIT

We utilized a variety of research equipment at this location, including a ghost box and copper dowsing rods. We captured audio (intelligent interactions), video, and photographic anomalies such as orbs, particularly around the area of a family burial mound. We experienced some camera phenomena while filming in the "den" area. The screen kept blurring periodically with what looked like a misty opaque presence, which I did not actually see with my eye, but it showed up on the screen. At the same time, although I did not see anything, I heard a muffled, shuffling-type noise in front of me. The camera acted as if it were trying to focus on something that was moving back and forth in front of it while I was trying to record Summer interacting with whatever spirit or entity might be there. A brand-new battery also drained quickly at that time.

Finally, we tested out the urban legend regarding spirits messing with cars parked in the front of the cemetery. People have reported coming back to their vehicle with the doors opened and the vehicle being moved back approximately five to six feet from the original parking space. When parking, we left the car doors unlocked and marked out lines under the tires to gauge the activity. Upon returning we did not observe any type of change or movement to the vehicle.

Notable points of interest in the cemetery are the Anderson family crypt, which features an artistic and detailed closure at the front of the mausoleum, and the "den," which was most likely an underground holding vault during the winters but is now left open to the elements.

DIRECTIONS

This cemetery is located off River Road, along an unmarked dirt road entrance diagonally across from Anderson Road in South Windham, Maine. You will see a rock wall along the road first, then a dirt road, which does not have signage and may appear as a driveway. Once you enter and start up the dirt road, you will see a clearing immediately in front of the graveyard that has space for parking and a gated entrance to the right. There is a sign there marked as "Anderson Cemetery."

ALSO NEARBY

Roam over to local favorite Cole Farms Restaurant and Pub. They've been in operation for over sixty-five years and boast home-cooked, family-type dining, and an outside picnic and playground area. Check out their menu and daily specials at www.colefarms.com.

Oriental Powder Company

WINDHAM, MAINE

27

SITE HISTORY

Two employees were blown to atoms.
—*New York Times,* February 8, 1901

The Oriental Powder Mills, also known as the Gambo Powder Mills, is located at the Gambo Falls on the Penobscot River in Windham, Maine. Built in 1824, it was the first and largest powder company in the state and the fourth largest in the entire country The workers made black powder for rifles, cannons, and explosives, and their contribution was invaluable to the Union Army during the Civil War. The 6,500 pounds a day the mill produced was twenty-five percent of all the gunpowder used in the conflict.

Producing gunpowder was dangerous work, and a total of thirty-two explosions were recorded at the mill. Countless workers were maimed or injured, and forty-five or forty-six men were killed in the explosions. So significant were the incidents that they made the *New York Times* on February 8, 1901, which stated, "Part of the Oriental Powder Mills at Newhall was demolished by an explosion early this forenoon. Two employees were blown to atoms. The cause of the explosion is unknown. There was about 2,000 pounds of powder in the building at the time, and the shock from the explosion was felt everywhere within a radius of a half-a-dozen miles."

Oriental Powder Company ruins in Windham, Maine.

Despite the dangers, workers were still easily found, since the mill paid nearly double the typical pay rate of similar jobs. The Oriental Powder Mills remained in operation for eighty years, outlasting all others in the state, but ultimately closed in 1905, after America's westward expansion pulled the demand away. The property was abandoned and the stone foundations, pathways, and canals left behind are viewable to this day. Plaques installed at the site detail the history of the site.

Left and right: Waterways at Oriental Powder Company.

DIRECTIONS

To get to the site, follow Gambo Road from Windham. When you reach the end of the road, you will find several parking spaces. Walk across the wooden bridge, and the three-quarter-mile looped path is on your left just after the bridge. Though the trail is an easy walk for most ages, care should taken due to some spots of uneven terrain.

ALSO NEARBY

In nearby Loveitt Cemetery you will find a plaque noting the many explosions at the mill, and the names of many of the men who lost their lives and are buried at the cemetery.

MAINE

28

Graves of the Captains

PORTLAND, MAINE

SITE HISTORY

I remember the sea fight far away,
How it thundered o'er the tide!
And the dead captains,
As they lay in their graves,
O'er looking the tranquil bay
where they in battle died.
And the sound of that mournful song
Goes through me with a thrill
A boy's will is the wind's will,
And the thoughts of youth are long, long thoughts.

—Henry Wadsworth Longfellow, "My Lost Youth"

During the War of 1812, the newly formed United States found itself at odds with the United Kingdom, and severe impediments to trade with the North American colonies were inflicted. A year into the war effort, little fighting of importance had been waged on Maine soil or sea. On September 5, 1813, however, the warfront reached Maine when the USS *Enterprise* spied the HMS *Boxer* chasing a small merchant ship off the coast of Pemaquid Point. The *Boxer* fired two shots toward the merchant ship, and though the *Enterprise* gave chase, they were forced to hang back when the *Boxer* slipped into Bath Harbor.

The graves of the captains.

Not to let these shots go unanswered, the *Enterprise* waited until it again spied the *Boxer*, this time off the coast of Monhegan Island. The *Enterprise*, with fourteen eighteen-pound carronades, two nine-pound long guns, and 102 men, bore down on the *Boxer* and its twelve eighteen-pound carronades, two nine-pound long guns, and sixty-six men. They both set anchor and prepared to fight, but calm winds kept the ships four miles apart for several hours, stalling the fight and heightening the tension. When the winds finally permitted closer proximity to their foes, Lieutenant Captain William Burrows of the *Enterprise* declared, "We are going to fight both ends and both sides of this ship as long as the ends and sides hold together," and so they did. The battle was won when the *Enterprise* raked the side of the *Boxer*, bringing down her mainmast, and all in all the loss to the *Enterprise* was four men killed and ten wounded, and seven were killed and thirteen were wounded on the *Boxer*. Though the *Enterprise* sustained damage to its rigging, it was able to keep the heavily hull-damaged *Boxer* afloat and towed it into Portland Harbor.

Though the *Enterprise* prevailed in the thirty-minute firefight that ensued, both Lieutenant Captain Burrows and the British Commander Samuel Blyth were mortally wounded. Though the dying lieutenant captain was offered Commander Blyth's sword in surrender, he denied it and elected to have it sent to his family, uttering, "I am satisfied; I die contented."

Portland, having only one horse-drawn carriage at the time, hastily painted another wagon black and draped it with fabric so that when the mahogany coffins were brought off the funeral barges, both Burrows and Blyth could be treated with appropriate dignity. Following a double funeral at the First Parish Meeting House, artillery companies on Munjoy Hill and cannons at Forts Prebble and Scammel honored the captains with a rousing salute as the procession made its way through the city.

The captains were buried side by side in Eastern Cemetery in Portland in raised box tombs with the following inscriptions:

CAPTAIN WILLIAM BURROWS

Beneath this stone moulders the body of Captain William Burrows, late commander of the United States Brig *Enterprise*, Who was mortally wounded on the 5th of September, 1813, in an action which contributed to increase the fame of American valor by capturing His Britannic Majesty's Brig *Boxer* after a severe contest of forty-five minutes, AEt. 28.

A passing stranger has erected this memorial of respect to the memory of a Patriot who in the hour of peril observed the loud summons of an injured, country , and who gallantly met, fought, and conquered," and . . .

Top: Eastern Cemetery gates. | Bottom: Eastern Cemetery.

CAPTAIN SAMUEL BLYTH

In memory of Captain Samuel Blyth, Late commander of His Britannic Majesty's Brig *Boxer*. He notably fell on the 5th day of September 1813, in action with the U.S. Brig *Enterprise*, In life honorable! In death glorious! His country will long deplore one of her bravest sons.

His friends long lament one of the best of men, AEt. 29. The surviving officers of his crew offer this feeble tribute of admiration and respect.

Two years later, Enterprise lieutenant Kevin Waters died from a wound inflicted at the battle and was interred in a third matching box grave with the following inscription:

LIEUTENANT KEVIN WATERS

Beneath this stone by the side of his gallant commander rest the remains of Lieutenant Kevin Waters. A native of Georgetown, District of Columbia, who received a mortal wound, September 5, 1813, while a midshipman on board the U.S. *Enterprise*.

In an action with his B.M. Brig *Boxer* which terminated in the capture of the latter. He languished in severe pain which he endured with fortitude until September 15, 1815 when he died with Christian calmness of resignation

AGED 18

The young men of Portland erect this stone as a testimony of their respect for his valor and virtues."

Unfortunately, years after the battle, additional information came to light that suggested that the merchant ship had actually paid the *Boxer* to provide them with an escort from Halifax to Bath. The cargo of the merchant ship was an illegal load of blankets and fabrics purchased from Canada, and the *Boxer* fired over the boat to give the impression that they were trying to enforce the trade restrictions. Unfortunately, the *Enterprise* was too convinced by the charade, and the battle commenced, with the loss of life perfectly avoidable. The captains are forever linked in history and in death.

DIRECTIONS

Eastern Cemetery, built by Portland's earliest settlers in 1668 and added to the National Register of Historic Places in 1973, is located at 224 Congress Street in Portland, Maine. Among over 700 stones and 4,000 interments with many early colonial designs are sections of varied religious and ethnic communities, including African American, Anglican, Quaker, and Puritan. Of particular note is the monument to Civil War hero Alonzo P. Stinson, fashioned in the shape of a military soldier's pack, and the original receiving tomb from 1849.

On-street parking is available on Congress and Mountfort Streets, with an ornate gate on the Congress Street side. Seasonal guided cemetery tours are offered three days a week from July through October by "Spirits Alive," a nonprofit organization focused on stone preservation and cemetery conservation of Eastern

Cemetery. Accessible year-round, a free map of the cemetery and its memorials can be picked up at the receiving tomb just inside the gates. Open dawn to dusk. More information can be obtained at www.spiritsalive.org.

ALSO NEARBY

When in the area, be sure to stop by Fort Allen Park on the Eastern Promenade at Fore Street. Located on a sixty-eight-acre landscape along Casco Bay, the site is home to the remains of the nineteenth-century fort and gun battery. The park itself, though the trails are not, is fully handicapped accessible with ample parking and provides viewing of lighthouses and Fort Gorges. Trail and park maps are available near the Fore Street entrance, and the park is open dawn to dusk.

International Cryptozoology Museum

PORTLAND, MAINE

SITE HISTORY

The International Cryptozoology Museum, recently relocated to 4 Thompson's Point Road, Suite 106, in Portland, Maine, is the epicenter of all things weird and mysterious. In fact, it's nearly impossible to miss and is easily spotted by a large, carved wooden Bigfoot outside its front door.

Cryptozoology, the study of hidden or unknown animals, usually focuses heavily on animals believed to exist but not yet having been confirmed by science, including Bigfoot, Yetis, sea serpents, and lake monsters. Visitors are informed of recently discovered evidence of new or previously considered extinct animals, such as coelacanth, megamouth sharks, Okapi, giant pandas, and mountain gorillas. The museum was designed and curated by internationally acclaimed cryptozoologist Dr. Loren Coleman, author of numerous works on the subject and consultant on many films, television programs, and field investigations.

The museum includes displays of foot casts and hair samples, and cryptozoological models from across the globe. Of particular note are actual hair samples from Abominable Snowmen, Yetis, Bigfoot, and Yowie; fecal matter from a Yeti; and an eight-foot-tall, 400-pound Bigfoot model, which are included in the over 10,000 items on exhibit. Displays on the Dover Demon, Jersey Devil, Montauk Monster, Feejee Mermaids, and Loch Ness Monster are also presented.

DIRECTIONS

The museum is open Wednesday through Monday and is handicapped accessible with ample parking. It is located in the Brick North building in suite number 106 at 4 Thompson's Point in Portland, Maine. Thompson's Point is adjacent to the Amtrak train and bus station. Due to frequent musical events and festivals at a concert venue on the property, it is recommended that you confirm the museum's hours by visiting www.cryptozoologymuseum.com.

ALSO NEARBY

After visiting the museum, grab a cocktail next door at the Stroudwater Distillery, made with small-batch house-made bourbon, rye, gin, and vodka, or sample a glass and learn about wine pairings at the nearby Cellar Door Winery.

MAINE

Candlemas Massacre

YORK, MAINE

SITE HISTORY

In the winter of 1692, villages along the New England coastline lived in constant fear of attack from Native Americans. It was the height of the conflict that came to be known as the Nine Year War, a series of six colonial wars between New France with their Native American allies and New England. In the early morning hours of January 24, 1692, the war descended on the small village of York, Maine, then known as part of the province of Massachusetts Bay.

Chief Madockawando, sachem of the Penobscot tribe, and Father Louis-Pierre Thury, a French missionary sent to serve as a Native American ally, led approximately 300 natives on a major raid of York. Before the sun rose that morning, every undefended home on the northern side of the York River, some seventeen or eighteen homes, were set ablaze; one hundred citizens were killed and another eighty-plus were taken captive and forced to march to Canada, where they were later ransomed when the war concluded.

Some of the victims included Reverend Shubael Dummer, who was shot on his own doorstep, then stripped naked, cut, and mangled nearly beyond recognition. Another was Joseph Moulton, the slain local tavern keeper, whose four-year-old son, Jeremiah, was one of the hostages taken, and who on his eventual release or escape from captivity became an important New England Militia officer. He enacted his revenge on the Native Americans who killed his family and destroyed his village by fighting in Father Rale's War. It was on a scouting expedition up the Kennebec River in 1724 that he earned the nickname as "the Indian Slayer."

A view of the Candlemas Massacre memorial.

A plaque now sits in the Old York Burying Ground on a rock on which the natives left their snowshoes before sneaking into town. The plaque gives a synopsis of the raid on York, and the town's historical society observes the anniversary of the event annually with costumed reenactments. Colonel Moulton is buried near the Raid on York / Candlemas Massacre Memorial.

Also located in the cemetery is the grave of Mary Nason, a local midwife who endured the undue reputation of being a "witch." When her husband buried her, he erected an elaborate tombstone featuring a woman's image and a "hog stone" to keep out wildlife, but urban legends quickly sprung up that the stone was meant to keep her from returning from the grave to haunt York and that her stone radiates heat. Though her stone is easily the most frequently visited in the cemetery, being covered with hundreds of coins and pebbles by visitors, it is also the most easily spotted in the cemetery, being the only grave that features the stone topper.

Jefferd's Tavern.

First Congregation Church in York, Maine.

DIRECTIONS

The Old York Burying Ground and the Old York Historical Society are located on the corner of Lindsay Road and York Road in York, Maine. Free on-site parking is available.

ALSO NEARBY

Directly across the street from the cemetery is the Old York Historical Society. On the grounds are Jefferd's Tavern, which is currently used as an event center, and the York Corner Schoolhouse. This 1755–1850 schoolhouse is open for self-guided tours and even features graffiti carved into the wood from students who attended the school hundreds of years ago. Detailed historical plaques and pamphlets are available and are placed nearby their related sites to allow for self-guided exploration of the historical sites.

MAINE

Amy Archer-Gilligan

WINDSOR, CONNECTICUT

31

SITE HISTORY

Patients caught in death trap convalescent home run by a quietly murderous nurse!

Amy Archer-Gilligan was the accused serial killer of the convalescing patients she cared for in her self-made nursing home, by way of systematic poisoning. Amy began her nursing-home career in the early 1900s, while living with her husband, James, and young daughter, Mary, in a Connecticut boardinghouse where she ran the business under the name "Sister Amy's Nursing Home for the Elderly." Later, when the owners decided to sell the boardinghouse, the Archers bought their own home in Windsor, Connecticut, and converted it into a nursing home. Unwittingly, the Archers may have pioneered the first for-profit nursing home in the United States, since there was previously no other known establishments of its kind.

There were a total of sixty deaths, both of men and women, between 1907 and 1917, in her nursing home on Prospect Street, with at least forty-eight of these suspicious deaths being attributed to Amy Archer. It seemed that Amy mostly targeted men for their money but did not hesitate to include women in her poisonous treatment if they got in the way or became suspicious of her. During investigations by law enforcement and family members, it was found that most of the victims had either recently handed over large amounts of money to Amy, named her as the sole beneficiary in their wills, or had new life insurance policies taken out on them by Archer a short time before their deaths.

Archer-Gilligan "Murder House" in Windsor, Connecticut.

Though it was known that Archer's customary imposed agreement for taking in patients was either to be named as beneficiary in the patient's will or to receive an initial payment of $1,000, the timing and suddenness of the patients' demise caused alarm to neighbors and family members. It was also the testimony of local store owners that Amy had routinely purchased large amounts of arsenic from their shops for unknown reasons. In the ensuing investigation, bodies of many of the deceased were exhumed and found to contain large amounts of arsenic in their systems.

Though her husband, James, seemed to have passed from natural causes, listed as Bright's disease on his death certificate, her second husband may not have been that lucky. One day in February 1914, Michael Gilligan had what was called an "acute bilious attack" and "severe indigestion," and he died suddenly. They had just married a few months prior, in 1913; his will left his entire estate to his wife, despite having four grown sons. The will was later found to be a forgery written by Amy herself.

Though twenty complaints had been brought against her by surviving family members, with five of those being prepared cases from the district attorney's office, she was ultimately tried and found guilty of only one murder, Franklin R. Andrews's, for which she was sentenced to life in prison. After spending just seven years at the Connecticut State Prison, she was deemed "insane" in 1924 and spent her remaining days at the Connecticut Hospital for the Insane in Middletown, Connecticut, until her death on April 23, 1962, in her early nineties.

DIRECTIONS

The former nursing home is located at 37 Prospect Street in Windsor, Connecticut. Since the current use of the building is unknown, it is recommended that you view the property from the sidewalk. Please do not disrupt the occupants or otherwise behave in a manner that would bring attention you would not desire brought to your own home. As always, the golden rule is the best rule.

The story of Amy Archer-Gilligan and her murderous deeds became the basis for the classic movie and stage play *Arsenic and Old Lace*. The play was originally written by Joseph Kesselring and was performed for the first time at the Fulton Theatre on Broadway in New York City in 1941. Later the movie version was created by Frank Capra and starred Cary Grant.

AUTHOR'S NOTE

The Archer-Gilligan house on Prospect Street in Windsor, Connecticut, remains nondescript, unassuming, and plain and looks nearly identical to news photos from the 1900s, minus the front porch, which you can see the imprint of where it was attached to the house. It does not have any type of signage or foliage or plants around it. It does have a bit of a "cold" feeling and is not at all homey. It's hard to determine whether it is being used as a residence or a historical site, but it is easily viewable and able to be photographed from the street. —S. G.

Gillette's Castle

EAST HADDAM, CONNECTICUT

32

SITE HISTORY

Born in Hartford, Connecticut, in 1853, William Gillette was an American stage actor who found fame and fortune portraying one of London's most famous fictional residents, Sherlock Holmes. Though he had achieved moderate success as an actor in Boston, New York, and the Midwest, it wasn't until he convinced Arthur Conan Doyle to allow him to adapt his iconic character for the stage that he became embedded in theater history. Over the course of his career, he portrayed Holmes over 1,300 times, including a film version in 1916, and is credited with giving the character his signature look: a deerstalker hat, cloak, curved pipe, and signature "Elementary" catch phrase.

With professional success came the funds necessary for Gillette to enjoy a bit of extravagance in his later life. In his case, a castle along the Seven Sisters section of the Connecticut River in East Haddam, Connecticut, on a 184-acre estate. Between 1914 and 1919, builders crafted the castle to reflect detailed plans of Gillette's own design. The twenty-two-room mansion featured forty-seven doors with unique locks on each, mirrors that allowed him to see most rooms in the house from his bedroom, and a secret hidden staircase in his study that allowed him freedom from unwanted visitors. The castle also included an art gallery, a library, and a small train that Gillette enjoyed driving around the property. One of his train engines remains on display in the visitor center.

Gillette Castle.

Gillette lived in his wonderful castle until his death in 1937, at which time his property was left to the state of Connecticut. The property is now referred to as Gillette Castle State Park and is open year-round for hiking and picnicking. Tours of the castle interior and the visitor center are open from 11:00 a.m. to 5:00 p.m. Thursday through Sunday from Memorial Day weekend through Labor Day. In-season camping sites are available.

AUTHOR'S NOTE

This was a particular treat to visit—the view was spectacular. It was what I pictured a smaller Winterfell from George R. R. Martin's *A Song of Ice and Fire* series to look like. The castle grounds and views were stunning, and I wished I had brought a meal to enjoy before departing. Make sure you take the time to take advantage of all the hiking and picnicking areas the park has to offer—it should be enjoyable all four seasons. —S. P.

DIRECTIONS

Gillette Castle State Park is located at 67 River Road in East Haddam, Connecticut. There is plenty of free parking available. Alternatively, spring through fall, you can travel to the castle across the Connecticut River on the historic Chester-Hadlyme Ferry, which has room for eight to nine cars. It can be picked up on Route 148 in Chester, Connecticut.

Top: Gillette Castle. | Bottom left: Train station.
Bottom Right: View of the Connecticut River, as seen from Gillette Castle.

33

Sandy Hook Elementary

NEWTOWN, CONNECTICUT

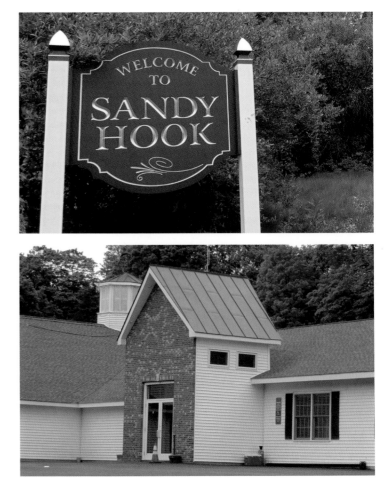

Top: Welcome sign upon entering the village of Sandy Hook in Newtown, Connecticut. | Bottom: Sandy Hook Volunteer Fire & Rescue, just beside Sandy Hook Elementary School.

SITE HISTORY

An unspeakably evil and deeply heartbreaking event took place at an elementary school in Newtown, Connecticut, on the morning of December 14, 2012. An angry and troubled young man, fully dressed for combat with multiple deadly, fully loaded weapons, walked up to the locked school entrance doors just after classes began and blasted through the protection glass with an assault rifle. He proceeded to walk through the corridor, stopping at the administrative and nurse's offices and shooting anyone he came across, before walking through the hall to the classrooms, shooting inside the rooms and executing both children and adults alike.

It took just five minutes for one person to systematically, brutally, and unapologetically murder twenty innocent first graders, the school principal, the school psychologist, and a teacher, with 154 rounds fired from two of the four weapons he had brought. The shooter also murdered his own mother before arriving at the school and then took his own life inside the school building.

To this day, there is still no clear understanding of the motive for these horrible actions. As well, the Internet is busy with conspiracy theories discussing the possibility that this event is not what authorities and the government report it to be. When you study the case, there are definitely more questions than answers surrounding this tragedy. Following this event was the shock, the

funerals, the memorials, the television coverage and interviews, the fundraisers to help the victims' families and community rebuild, the investigations, and the heightened awareness to this country's issues with gun control and mental illness.

The imprinted memory here is that there were six adults and twenty pure little souls taken from the families of Newtown. One cannot imagine how difficult a journey to healing that must be.

Almost immediately, an initiative was begun to memorialize the lives of the victims and build playgrounds in areas damaged by Hurricane Sandy. There are twenty-six locations dedicated to the twenty-six adults and children lost to this tragedy. The concept was created by William "Bill" Lavin, an experienced firefighter, who had worked in assisting his home community of Elizabeth, New Jersey, repair the damage from Hurricane Sandy in 2012. In the aftermath of the Newtown event, he founded Sandy Ground Project and worked with the Where Angels Play Foundation to make it all happen. As of 2015, all twenty-six playgrounds have been completed throughout the coastal areas of Connecticut, New York, and New Jersey. A listing of all playground sites can be found at www.whereangelsplayfoundation.org.

AUTHOR'S NOTE

We visited the elementary school, the gravesite for Victoria Soto, and two of the dedicated playgrounds. Visiting the site of Sandy Hook Elementary prior to completion of the new construction was an incredibly sad and sobering moment. It is located on the same road as the local fire department that served as the main headquarters for parents, investigators, and emergency personnel during the aftermath of this tragic event. The world saw this building in the background on news channels as the event was unfolding. We had hoped for a peek at the new construction going on, but the entire school grounds was surrounded by an eight- to ten-foot-tall chain-link privacy fence that you could not see through. The only thing visible was a crane boom and the tops of other construction equipment. There were signs warning of "no trespassing" and that the entrance was for "personnel only." The construction has since been completed and the school opened for the 2016–2017 school year for kindergarten through fourth-grade students.

Top: Victoria Soto Park in Stratford, Connecticut.
Bottom: Victoria Soto's gravestone at Union Cemetery in Stratford.

The park sites of Victoria Soto and Josephine Gay were beautiful tributes to each of those victims and give a wonderful place for children to play, enjoy nature's beauty, and be free from harm. Victoria Leigh "Vicki" Soto was the twenty-seven-year-old teacher of a first-grade class at Sandy Hook Elementary School. She was one of the six staff members killed in the tragedy. She had done everything in her immediate power to protect all of the children in her classroom by hiding them in closets and various concealed areas and telling the gunman that they were not in the classroom as he entered, and then finally she had thrown herself in front of some of the children who had tried to flee in terror, in order to shield them from the close-range gunfire. Miss Soto's memorial playground, in Stratford, Connecticut, is a celebration of her life and is decorated with many of her favorite things, such as pink flamingos, the color hot pink, a sign-language chart, and a fully ornamented and lighted Christmas tree. Victoria Soto's gravesite at Union Cemetery is similarly decorated, with a large flamingo engraved on her stone and many trinkets and tributes left for her that again proved that she was well loved by family, friends, and her students and had touched many lives in her short twenty-seven years.

Josephine "Joey" Gay was a first grader at Sandy Hook Elementary School at the time of the shooting and had just turned seven years old three days prior to the tragedy. Joey was the youngest of three children, all girls, and was a special-needs child diagnosed with autism. Her family remembers her as a joyful spirit with a beautiful smile who loved peanut butter and the color purple. Her family started Joey's Fund under the Doug Flutie Jr. Foundation for Autism, which awards grants to people with autism and their families. Joey's playground is built right on the beach at Seaside Park in Bridgeport, Connecticut, and is painted purple in her honor. The family's wish is for children and families to enjoy the beauty of the ocean and peaceful surroundings of this playground in memory of Joey.

Josephine "Joey" Gray's Playground at Seaside Park in Bridgeport, Connecticut.

DIRECTIONS

Sandy Hook Elementary School is located at 12 Dickinson Drive, Sandy Hook, Connecticut.

Victoria Soto's grave is located at Union Cemetery in Stratford, Connecticut. Upon entering at the main entrance on Temple Court, take the path to the left of the Union Cemetery sign, then proceed straight ahead. Ms. Soto's grave is located on the left in Section K, which is marked on a tree on the left-hand side. Victoria Soto Park is the fifth Where Angels Play / Sandy Ground Project park that was completed and is located next to Pender's Field at Longbrook Park, on the corners of Glendale and Charlton Streets in Stratford, Connecticut.

Josephine Gay's Playground is the sixth Where Angels Play / Sandy Ground Project park that was completed and is located at Seaside Park at the South End of Bridgeport, Connecticut. There are restrooms, handicapped parking, park benches, and picnic tables available at both of these playground sites.

Ed and Lorraine Warren

BRIDGEPORT, SOUTHINGTON, AND MONROE, CONNECTICUT

SITE HISTORY

Anyone who even remotely follows the paranormal world has undoubtedly heard of the supernatural investigative couple Ed and Lorraine Warren. In their active days, they were prolific in reputation as well as in their investigations, subsequent writings, and mentoring of other paranormal investigators. They have written a book series based on their experiences, have made numerous appearances on local and national TV shows and documentaries, and have consulted on movie productions as well as appeared in movie cameos.

Mr. Warren was a military veteran and former police officer and, sadly, passed in 2008. Mrs. Warren had been educated in Catholic schools and noticed but didn't fully understand her gift of sensitivity to energies at a very young age. She is still living and resides in Monroe, Connecticut. The Warrens started out together in their home state of Connecticut, becoming self-taught in the paranormal and investigating manifestations and began specializing in demonology. In 1952, the Warrens created the New England Society for Paranormal Research (NESPR) as a base for their efforts in supernatural education and investigation. The Warrens claim to have investigated thousands of cases. They opened themselves up to sharing their experience and knowledge in an effort to help people who were experiencing hauntings, possessions, or otherwise strange ghostly or demonic activity. It is important to note that both of the Warrens came from a strong, God-fearing Catholic faith, which played into why they wanted to help those who may have been experiencing supernatural and unholy terrorism.

Ed Warren's final resting place at Stepney Cemetery, Monroe, Connecticut.

Some of their more well-known cases are the Snedecker Demon House, the Perron Family haunting (on which the movie *The Conjuring* is based), the Annabelle doll, the Enfield poltergeist in England, the Smurl haunting in Pennsylvania, and the Amityville house in Long Island, New York. There are also many, many lesser-known cases they have investigated local to Connecticut. The Warrens created a museum, located in their own home, of haunted things that they had acquired, such as items and artifacts that have been known to be possessed or otherwise negatively affected by entities. They believed that the items should be controlled and contained rather than destroyed, since this would release the dwelling, evil spirits to be able to manifest and attach to other items.

AUTHOR'S NOTE

ED WARREN'S GRAVE AT STEPNEY CEMETERY

We made the trek to Ed and Lorraine Warren's home town of Monroe, Connecticut, and visited Ed's grave at Stepney Cemetery. Mr. Warren passed away at home with his wife, Lorraine, by his side on August 23, 2008. At the start of the visit to the cemetery we did encounter a bit of weirdness, as a clergyman, dressed in a dark-brown-burlap, monk-type robe and clutching a very large wooden rosary in his hands, walked out of the back of the church that is located next to the cemetery, and began strolling through the cemetery in prayer.

After we parked and began walking down the main path, we saw a man sitting on a stone bench in front of a headstone, sobbing uncontrollably into his cupped hands covering his face. We were immediately struck with the feeling of overwhelming sadness and quickly took a path away from him so as not to disturb him.

At this point, we were in the center of the cemetery, so Summer decided to do a little test with me and let me follow my gut as to where Ed's grave was located (I had never been there before, but she had). As she hung back and videotaped, I definitely felt guided and pulled in a certain direction, and I was able to walk straight to the grave. The moment I realized that I had arrived exactly in front of the big, black-marble obelisk-like stone with the name "Warren" etched on it, I was pretty amused and amazed with myself!

Now, how Mr. Warren felt about that is another story. We got the sense that he wasn't too amazed or amused. We began getting vibes, messages, and feelings immediately upon entering the cemetery, and as soon as we turned on the audio and video recorders at Ed's grave we started communicating with more than one entity. We believe one of these entities was Ed Warren. There did seem to be multiple spirits trying to communicate with us; we noted different voices and demeanors. Ed showed up right away, answering most of our questions in short, curt replies. He is in Spirit as he was in real life, "very matter of fact." We confirmed that it was him by asking the standard confirmation questions and establishing a baseline. He seemed annoyed and abrupt. Toward the middle to end of the conversation, he made several comments to us, such as "we weren't worth it," "go now," and "good-bye." Talk about an ego deflator (us) or an inflated ego (Ed)!

At least one of the other entities seemed more gentle and made comments that seemed to be directed at Ed to the effect of "taking it easy" or "calming down." We made a final request for him to please communicate to Lorraine (still living) that we said "Hello," to which he agreed by stating, "Lorraine approves." Please check out our video and audio recording of this visit posted on our YouTube site at www.youtube.com/ScaryNewEngland.

THE BRIDGEPORT POLTERGEIST HOUSE

The plain, tiny bungalow house at 966 Lindley Street in Bridgeport, Connecticut, is the site of what is said to be the most documented poltergeist haunting ever. It is intriguing, since accounts were recorded and offered by multiple legitimate witnesses such as law enforcement, friends, journalists, and other investigators. The story involved very active, peculiar, and frightening poltergeist activity, sometimes turning violent. The activity soon seemed to surround the family's young adopted daughter, Marcia Goodin, who was an eleven-year-old Five Nations Indian from Ontario, Canada. She had fallen ill and was housebound for many weeks, during which time many of the incidents took place. When the story broke publicly, there ensued a media frenzy, and many thousands of people eventually made their rounds to Lindley Street to gawk at the home. Although many of the incidents were closely witnessed and collaborated by the likes of police officers, firefighters, emergency personnel, and the investigators allowed into the home, the city authorities of Bridgeport wanted the negative activity to stop and so declared it a "hoax." Later, those who were at the scene, such as the Warrens and Mr. Paul Eno, have detailed their accounts in books.

The house today sits unassuming and quiet, not outwardly updated at all from the era in which it was built; the only protection from outsiders is a old chain-link fence, and parking is streetside. It does seem to be currently occupied by the living. At fifty-one years of age, Marsha Godin (changed from Marcia Goodin) died of natural causes at OhioHealth MedCentral Hospital in Shelby, Richland County, Ohio, on February 10, 2015.

THE SNEDECKER DEMON HOUSE

This home on Meriden Road in Southington, Connecticut, is the site of the much-debated and possibly most elaborate hoax in "haunted history" but is a story that resulted in a major motion picture. This tale starts out as a family searching for a home closer to the medical facility in Connecticut where their sick son was being treated. They find what they believe is the perfect home, a duplex with plenty of room for their immediate and extended family, only twenty minutes from the hospital. They are soon creeped out by the revelation that the house used to be a funeral home, and each member of the family was methodically terrorized and even reportedly sodomized by unseen entities! The horrific haunting went on for two years before the adults decided to pack up the children and get on the road to a nonhaunted, not-formerly-a-funeral-home kind of house.

Snedecker Demon House in Southington, Connecticut.

During and immediately after the family lived in this home, naysayers reported that none of the events that the family had recounted had actually happened. It was a very much publicized case at the time, with a whole *Sally Jessy Raphael* special devoted to the story, along with interviews, news stories, articles, books, and eventually a motion picture and TV movies devoted to telling the family's story. It seems that only the family members know what really happened during those two years they lived at 208 Meriden Road. Sadly, the Snedeckers' son, who was so sick at the time, did pass away from his illnesses a few years back, but only after growing up and enjoying a family of his own. The home today looks almost exactly the same as it did back then, and the neighborhood seemed quiet and family oriented on the day that we took our streetside pictures.

DIRECTIONS

Ed Warren's grave is located at Stepney Cemetery in Monroe, Connecticut. His grave is toward the front of the cemetery along the side closest to the treeline. It is a large black obelisk and should be easily spotted as you enter the grounds. The Bridgeport Poltergeist House is located at 966 Lindley Street in Bridgeport, Connecticut, and the Snedecker Demon House is located at 208 Meriden Road in Southington, Connecticut.

Center Church on the Green

NEW HAVEN, CONNECTICUT

35

SITE HISTORY

In a moment, in the twinkling of an eye, at the last trump, the dead shall be raised.

—Center Church on the Green Plaque

THE CHURCH

Center Church on the Green is a National Historic Landmark in downtown New Haven, Connecticut. Founded in 1638 by Reverend John Davenport, the congregation comprised a small group of Puritans from the Boston area who had settled in the area. The fourth meetinghouse to be built on the Green, this ornate building was designed and built by Ithiel Towne between 1812 and 1814.

A large brick steeple adorns the structure, but the true beauty lies within the worship space. With high ceilings, elaborate chandeliers, and a Fisk organ with 2,582 pipes, the focal point of the church is an exquisite 2,320-piece Tiffany window memorializing Reverend Davenport's first sermon to his flock.

Eli Whitney, inventor of the cotton gin, was the regular occupant of pew 63, and Daniel Webster held a rousing rally on current politics there in 1837. Many notable visitors also came to worship at the church—notably President James Monroe in 1817 and President Rutherford B. Hayes in 1870, who always paid his respects to family members buried in the crypt below the church.

Top: The original church sign, pulpit, and stained glass window at Center Church, New Haven, Connecticut. | Bottom: The basement crypt holds the remains of many of the first parishioners of the church.

THE CRYPT

When the church was constructed the Upper Green was used as a public cemetery, containing the remains of 5,000 to 10,000 early settlers of the New Haven Colony. The church was built over a small portion of the cemetery, with 137 identified plots left in their original positions. The foundation of the church was carefully built around the slate, granite, and brownstone gravestones, tables, and box tombs, ranging in date from 1687 to 1812. In addition to the identified plots, the church estimates that there are likely an additional 1,000 unmarked graves in the small space.

In 1821, the remaining stones and monuments outside the bounds of the foundation were moved to nearby Grove Cemetery, though the bodies were not disinterred and remain there in unmarked graves to this day.

In 1880, parishioner Henry Trowbridge Jr. drew a complete layout of the crypt, which is on display and available in paper form to assist in identifying the plots in the crypt, including Benedict Arnold's first wife. A serious water issue has resulted because of a concrete floor that was keeping moisture trapped against the gravestones and, compounded with the natural aging over time, has led to significant deterioration. In 1987, the concrete was replaced with unmortared bricks, and though this has been a marked improvement, many of the stones remain in need of stabilization repairs. To that end, the New Haven Crypt Restoration Committee encourages volunteers and tax-deductible donations and sells souvenirs to aid in the preservation efforts.

Left: Center Church exterior with steeple.
Right: Amistad Memorial.

DIRECTIONS

The church and crypt are located at 250 Temple Street in New Haven, Connecticut. Crypt visiting hours are held April through October from 11:00 a.m. to 1:00 p.m. on Saturdays. Appointments should be made for large groups due to the size of the space and the need for care in maneuvering around. The crypt is accessed by a steep and narrow staircase and is not handicapped accessible. On-street metered parking is available on the streets surrounding the Green. An "Open and Affirming Christian Church," the United Church of Christ holds weekly Sunday services that are open to all. More information can be accessed at http://centerchurchonthegreen.org/.

ALSO NEARBY

You can view some of the stones that were removed from the Upper Green at Grove Street Cemetery, located at the corner of Grove and Prospect Streets. Free docent-guided tours of the cemetery are available, leaving from the chapel / cemetery office, just inside the main gate, at 11:00 a.m. on Saturday and noon on Sunday. The stones from New Haven Green are easily viewed year-round, arranged in alphabetical order resting around the west and north interior cemetery walls, and printed self-guided tour information is available at their website at www.greenstreetcemetery.org.

Also visit the Amistad Memorial, which is viewable outside New Haven City Hall on the Church Street side of the Green, at the site at the former jail where the slaves accused of mutiny on the La Amistad ship were held.

36

Graves of P. T. Barnum and General Tom Thumb

BRIDGEPORT, CONNECTICUT

SITE HISTORY

There's a sucker born every minute.

—P. T. Barnum

Phineas Taylor Barnum was known as the "Prince of Humbug," a title he embraced wholeheartedly. He felt that a little "humbug," something presented with the intent to deceive and mislead, was warranted as long as the consumers were getting entertainment value for their money. The consummate businessman believed "the bigger the humbug, the better people like it," and his reputation as the most famous showman of all time continues to this day.

P. T. Barnum was born in Bethel, Connecticut, in July 1810. His early career prospects included running a general store, publishing a weekly newspaper, and, most successfully, operating a Connecticut-wide lottery. However, when the state made the lotteries illegal in 1834, he sold the store and newspaper and moved his family to New York, where he began his career as the noted showman he was destined to become.

He purchased a blind slave woman named Joice Heth from promoter R. W. Lindsay and claimed that she was the 160-year-old former nurse of George Washington. He purchased a failing museum in 1841 and reopened it with the name of "Barnum's American Museum," featuring a wax museum, zoo, and freak show. His first humbug at the museum was the "FeeJee Mermaid," which he had manufactured by a local taxidermist from a fish's tail and the torso and head of a monkey, which he presented as a real creature. After his museum burned down twice, in 1865 and 1868, he decided to abandon the museum business and take his

The Barnum family plot at Mountain Grove Cemetery in Bridgeport.

creations on the road as "the Greatest Show on Earth," later partnering with James Bailey to create America's first three-ring circus.

One of Barnum's star performers was the diminutive Charles Sherwood Stratton. Barnum met Stratton and gave him the stage name of "General Tom Thumb" when he was five years old, teaching him to sing, dance, and do celebrity impressions. Though Stratton was born and grew typically for the first six months of his life, his full adult height maxed out at three foot four inches tall. With a personality that was far larger than life, he was immediately successfully received on tours across the country and later in Europe, where he performed for Queen Victoria twice. He died suddenly of a stroke in 1883 at the age of forty-five, and Barnum had a life-sized statue of Stratton to adorn his final resting place in Mountain Grove Cemetery in Bridgeport, Connecticut. While his funeral was attended by over 20,000 friends and admirers, the unique headstone also drew some unwanted attention. In 1959, a group of unidentified vandals stole and smashed the statue causing significant damage to both the statue and the headstone itself. After an outpouring of public support and many fundraisers, the Barnum Festival Society and the Mountain Grove Cemetery Association were able to have the statue replaced and the stone repaired.

After suffering a stroke of his own during a performance in 1890, Barnum later passed away on April 7, 1891, at the age of eighty. He bequeathed the skeletal remains of Jumbo the Elephant from his circus to the American Museum of Natural History and his hind to Tufts University. The remainder of his displays he had toured the country with, including his FeeJee Mermaid, were donated to the city of Bridgeport, where he had served as mayor for one year. The city opened the "Barnum Institute of Science and History" in 1893. The building, listed on the National Register of Historic Places, features some of P. T. Barnum's and Tom Thumb's belongings and humbugs as well as Pa-Ib the Mummy, which was authenticated after his death.

In December of 2017, *The Greatest Showman*, a musical loosely based on Barnum's life was released. Starting Hugh Jackman in the lead role, the film presents a much more likable version of Barnum than was probably accurate and ignores some of his less family-friendly ventures, such as the black-faced minstrel acts featured in some of his earlier productions. What it does provide in spades is a strong score by the Oscar-winning duo of Benj Pasek and Justin Paul. Every song is a showstopper and the Bearded Lady's anthem "This is Me" has been nominated for both Golden Globes and Academy Awards.

AUTHOR'S NOTE

I find it interesting to note that for a man who was so decidedly desiring of attention and who did everything in larger-than-life grandeur that his grave is marked with such an understated tombstone. The family plot simply states: "NOT MY WILL BUT THINE BE DONE." The quiet serene setting and reserved stone does not seem as showy as would be expected, but maybe ultimately well suited for the man who famously said, "I don't care what they say about me, just make sure they spell my name right!" —S. P.

P. T. Barnum statue at Seaside Park in Bridgeport, Connecticut.

The life-sized statue attop General Tom Thumb/Charles Stratton's gravestone.

The Barnum Museum.

DIRECTIONS

P. T. Barnum and Charles Stratton are buried near each other in Mountain Grove Cemetery at 2675 North Avenue in Bridgeport, Connecticut. If you drive through the main gates, follow the road ahead of you nearly to the rear of the cemetery. You will easily be able to spot the life-sized model of Stratton perched on an obelisk on the right side of the road. While standing in front of Stratton's final resting place, orient yourself to face the same direction that he is looking, and you will find Barnum's understated stone approximately one hundred feet away on the other side of the road, partially obscured by some bushes.

ALSO NEARBY

The Barnum Museum is located at 820 Main Street in Bridgeport, Connecticut, and is a must-see spot when in the area. However, due to continuing renovations stemming from fifteen million dollars of damage that the museum sustained in a freak tornado hitting the building in June 2010, their hours should be confirmed by visiting www.barnum-museum.org or calling 203-331-1104, ext. 100, prior to planning your visit. On-street parking is available.

Additionally, a statue of P. T. Barnum was commissioned by the city of Bridgeport and was installed at Seaside Park at 1 Barnum Dyke, overlooking the Long Island Sound. The park also offers sports fields, playgrounds, and beach access for swimming and picnicking.

American Stigmata

WOONSOCKET, RHODE ISLAND

SITE HISTORY

My heart bleeds under the weight of suffering, but my will remains united to Thine, and I cry out to Thee: Lord it is for them that I want to suffer . . . I wish to mingle my tears with Thy Precious Blood for that salvation of those I love . . .

—Little Rose Marie Feron

Marie Rose Ferron, "Little Rose," was born on May 24, 1902, in a stable in St. Germain de Grantham, Quebec, Canada. The tenth of fifteen children in a pious Catholic family, she was described by all who met her as very precocious both in her intelligence and piety.

Her devotion for Jesus and his followers became pronounced at the age of three, when she took a particular liking for St. Anthony of Padua. If someone in her large household lost something, she claimed to invoke the assistance of her favorite saint and, with his help, always seemed to be able to find what was missing.

Though a devout Catholic himself, Little Rose's father became annoyed by her fixation and decided to teach her a lesson. One day he came home from work and hid his boots on the other side of the railroad tracks near their home. He asked her to hand him his boots, and she promptly got on her coat and went out and retrieved them. Her father never doubted her religious enthusiasm again.

American stigmatist Marie Rose Ferron's grave.

Precious Blood Cemetery in Woonsocket, Rhode Island.

At the age of six, the Ferrons relocated to Fall River, Massachusetts. It was there that Little Rose had her first vision of Jesus, carrying a cross. She instantly declared an intent to become a nun, but at age thirteen she was stricken by a mysterious illness that caused paralysis and painful contractions of muscles in her legs, feet, arms, and hands, requiring her to walk with crutches. Several years passed and her illness progressed and her feet became clubbed, and she was confined to bed for the rest of her life. She also battled with digestive issues and intestinal problems, which severely limited her ability to eat solid foods, as well as tetanus and pyorrhea, which required tooth extractions and the installation of a metal plate in her mouth.

In 1925, at the age of twenty-two, the family moved one final time to Woonsocket, Rhode Island.

One year later, Little Rose showed signs of the marks corresponding to those left on Jesus's body by crucifixion, known as stigmata. Little Rose was considered a "Victim Soul," taking on the bodily suffering in reparation for the sins of others and to heal those in need. She began bleeding from her eyes and forehead, which also displayed heavy swelling of the flesh on her forehead in bands surrounding her head, a four-inch wound on her side, bruised blotches all over her body, and wounds on both sides of her hands. Photographs taken of Little Rose have documented and supported these events and were verified by members of the Franco-American Catholic and medical communities. She also experienced "ecstasies" in which she was said to have been given visions and conversations with Jesus and Mary, where she was heard praying and singing, most often in French. In time, Marie Rose resigned herself to God's will, and she accepted her sickness as her vocation and even felt privileged to be chosen to do so.

Though she was able to move only two of her fingers and her mouth toward the end of her life, she kept herself busy making crafts, including bookmarks, braids, and rosaries, stating that her "Little Jesus wants me to work." Throughout her suffering, thousands of devotees flocked to her bedside to pray with her. Busloads of people from all over the country were received at the home of America's only stigmatic.

She was not free from criticism, however, and was the brunt of gossip and ridicule. Former friends started rumors that she was eating steak dinners with her parents and going for walks around Woonsocket under the cover of darkness, and that she was using concealed pins to cause the stigmata marks. Devotees are quick to draw parallels to Judas's betrayal of Christ.

Many chose to believe the false rumors, and in 1964, Bishop Russell McVinney released a decree indicating that he didn't believe that she met the standards of the Catholic church for canonization. In response, Reverend John Baptist Palm interviewed hundreds of people on tape about Little Rose's extraordinary and heroic ventures, publishing them in the book *Tape Recorded Little Rose Testimonies* and sending a copy to every bishop in the United States. He hand-delivered copies to the bishops in Providence, hoping that by giving them the "incontestable evidence of her heroic ventures of Marie Rose Ferron" it might help to open the way for the cause. Unfortunately, they remained unmoved, with the Reverend Monsignor Paul D. Theroux noting that, "It would seem that Little Rose was indeed a very spiritual person, and quite possibly one of the many unheralded Saints" and that "many have been inspired by her example of Christian Suffering" that they "simply do not have sufficient evidence to meet the requirements for a formal cause for Sainthood." The cause is not yet lost, however, with the Ukrainian Autocephalous Orthodox Church of America glorifying her and raising her to a saint within their jurisdiction and making a public commitment to continue to fight for the recognition Little Rose so suffered for.

When Little Rose passed away on May 11, 1936, she was thirty-three years old, the same age as Jesus was when he was crucified. During her funeral services, thousands filed past her body paying their respects, and nearly 15,000 signed the guest book. An editorial in the local paper noted:

> There are things one can never forget;
> for us it is the radiant face of Rose Ferron. She was
> beautiful, but hers was not a natural beauty, but rather
> a mystifying one: a slight luminous emanation seemed
> to escape continually from that angelic face.

AUTHOR'S NOTE

I visited Precious Blood Cemetery on an early-fall afternoon and was instantly taken by the serenity and beauty of the grounds. Though the cemetery is nestled in the heart of a city of over 41,000 citizens, it holds none of the trappings of the typical urban burial ground and seems removed from the noise and hustle and bustle of city living. The plots are well spaced and arranged with many large tombs, monuments, and sculptures arranged throughout. Visitors to the area are encouraged to allow some time to wander the grounds and view some of the most ornate displays of Catholic art that I have ever viewed. — S. P.

An ornate monument in Precious Blood Cemetery in Woonsocket, Rhode Island.

DIRECTIONS

Marie Rose Ferron is buried in Precious Blood Cemetery on Diamond Hill Road in Woonsocket, Rhode Island. As you enter the cemetery gates, bear to the right and follow the road a short distance to the first intersection. Stop there, and you will find Little Rose's final resting spot on the left-hand side of the road, two plots down from the corner. Her white-marble stone lies flat on the ground and features a highly detailed engraving of religious symbolism, including a cross, a crown of thorns, and a dove of peace. Her stone, when translated from French, describes her as "The Little Rose, victim of her Jesus, Marie Rose Ferron, Stigmatist."

Slater Mill

PAWTUCKET, RHODE ISLAND

SITE HISTORY

Born in Derbyshire, England, in 1768, Samuel Slater was one of eight children of a successful farmer and landowner. Desiring a different life than his father before him, he took an apprenticeship under Jedediah Strutt, a partner of noted British inventor Sir Richard Arkwright. He studied hard and learned all facets of the cotton-manufacturing business, working his way up to supervisor of Strutt Mill. He longed to relocate to the United States, but Britain wanted to maintain its world monopoly on textile production and prohibited the exportation of machinery or the emigration of individuals with mechanical knowledge. Slater knew his proficiency and expertise were valuable, and he left England in disguise and under the cover of darkness, arriving in New York City in 1789.

There he met Moses Brown, a prominent Rhode Island Quaker merchant, who agreed to finance a business venture using Slater's precisely memorized specifications for equipment to open a small mill in Providence in 1790. In 1793, the duo moved their operation to Pawtucket, and when they successfully spun cotton thread, they became the first profitable waterpowered mill in America, The forty-three-by-twenty-nine-foot, two-story mill powered by water flowing from the nearby Blackstone River employed children ages six to twelve who could get inside the dangerous looming machine without the costs associated with stopping it for repairs.

Top: The Slater Mill, which doubles as a visitor center and gift shop.
Bottom: The waterwheel inside the Wilkinson Mill.

Slater eventually owned mills in several states and became one of America's leading industrialists, and President Andrew Jackson dubbed him "the Father of the American Industrial Revolution." He was also credited with what came to be called "the Rhode Island Method"—the practice of hiring whole families, adults and children alike, to work in his mills while living in company housing, shopping in company-owned stores, and studying in company-owned schools. Remnants of these workers are still visible throughout the mill complex on the actual original equipment still present: the initials of former workers were carved on some of this equipment, and a single, small, blackened, child-sized handprint is visible on a main floor beam.

An example of the kind of housing used by mill families is still present just outside the Slater Mill, appropriately named the Sylvanus Brown House. Built in 1758, it was originally located across the Blackstone River but was relocated to the mill complex to make way for an expansion of the I-95 highway. Maintained as a typical artisan house of the period, the building was occupied by Sylvanus Brown, who was a woodworker, millwright, dam builder, and pattern maker who made patterns for Slater's early textile machines. In addition to a large spice and herb garden behind it, the displays inside the house include relics of pre-industrial-era home-based textile looms that provide an interesting contrast to the large machines in the mills next door.

Just beside the Brown House is the five-story rubble-stone-walled Wilkinson Mill. Oziel Wilkinson, a blacksmith of nails and anchors, built the massive structure in 1810 with three-foot-thick walls and a 16,000-pound waterwheel. The wheel turns as water from the river flows into the millrace, which in turn powers the shafts that turn the gears in the machinery shop above. The father-in-law of Slater, who was married to Oziel's daughter Hannah, the all-male crew cast the iron for Slater's cotton-carding machines. When weather conditions are right, the wheel is still operational, and the machines can still be run.

As the site of early industry, the mill experienced its share of related unfortunate mishaps, and many deaths occurred on the property, earning it a reputation as one of the most haunted places in America. In addition to being featured on many paranormal television programs, including SyFy's *Ghost Hunters*, the mill

Interior of the Wilkinson Mill.

regularly holds its own "Mills and Mysteries Paranormal Investigations" led by renowned paranormal expert, demonologist, and Slater Mill interpreter (tour guide) Carl L. Johnson. Johnson regales visitors with tales of haunts, including a seven-year-old little girl who resides in the Sylvanus Brown House, the full-bodied apparition of Samuel Slater wandering the whole complex, picture anomalies, EVPs, disembodied voices, and even physical contact and object manipulation by unseen hands.

Through a combination of the wheel in Wilkinson Mill churning the high-mineral-content water from the river and giving the space a low-level electrical charge thought to allow spirits to manifest, as well as absorbed energy in the wood and stone created by hundreds of individuals having worked decades in the mill, it seems that some have chosen to remain. A mixture both of residual and intelligent haunts have been reported, and though they do not guarantee that you will have your own ghostly encounter, the staff claims that it's rare that the spirits of Slater Mill don't make their presence known.

AUTHOR'S NOTE

I visited Slater Mill on a bright summer day, but this did nothing to diminish my desire to seek out the more paranormal aspects of its history. I lucked out when I arrived and found Carl about to begin a tour of the property. Since I was alone on this adventure, I joined a family with several small children, and we began our tour of the Brown House. As we went through the home, Carl noted in passing that the resident spirit was just about the same age as one of the girls on the tour. She loudly squealed and there was a faint but distinct giggle behind me. Not being familiar with the acoustics of the building, I shrugged it off and made note that I wasn't going to be able to ask my questions of Carl while the children were in earshot.

We continued through into the Wilkinson Mill, and I was instantly impressed by how notably different the vibe was. The waterwheel was massive, and the water made the room seem to lightly hum. When we made our way upstairs, we entered the machine shop, and it instantly felt as if dozens of eyes were upon us. I frequently straggle along behind a tour group to take pictures unobstructed and was taking a shot of a sign that warned against loafing, and after several shots of the sign I felt a gruff tug on my backpack toward the rest of the group. It was clear someone did not want me to dawdle behind.

After a quick walk along the river, we entered the Slater Mill, and I again encountered a change in the feeling. Whereas Wilkinson Mill felt very masculine and as if I was trespassing, in Slater Mill I felt instantly welcome. It was easy to envision all of the small children who had worked there, and the machinery was impressive in scale. When Carl (quite delicately, I might note) told our group about how many children were maimed or killed while working in the still-running machines, he turned one of the more foreboding ones on. I involuntarily took a step back and whispered, "Those poor children." Just a moment later, I felt a pair of reassuring hands reach around my waist, causing the backup camera in my bag to bang against my back with no one standing near me to have done so.

When the tour concluded, I pulled Carl aside, safely out of earshot of the children, and shared my experiences with him. He confirmed that they were perfectly on par with the kinds of experiences he and his fellow interpreters have had. I eagerly anticipate making a return trip to the mills to partake in a nighttime investigation. It's well worth a visit, at any hour. —S. P.

DIRECTIONS

The historic Slater Mill Complex is located at 67 Roosevelt Avenue in Pawtucket, Rhode Island. The complex is not handicapped accessible in many areas due to stairs. Hours vary by season, with many special arts, music, and cultural events in addition to their paranormal investigations, and meeting rooms can be reserved for functions. They can be reached by phone 401-725-8638 or online at www.slatermill.org.

Exterior of the Wilkinson Mill.

39

Swan Point Cemetery

PROVIDENCE, RHODE ISLAND

SITE HISTORY

Swan Point Cemetery, at 585 Blackstone Street in Providence, Rhode Island, is a National Historic Landmark. The nondenominational garden-style cemetery, spread over 200 acres of hills and rivers, is well landscaped and a pleasant place to go for a walk. A kiosk housing an interment site location computer is located in the vestibule of the administrative building; the computer has a self-service touchscreen, allowing searches by name and printouts of detailed maps.

JOHN ROGERS VINTON

Of the many interments of interest at Swan Point was the first military burial in the cemetery in 1847. A native son of Providence, Rhode Island, born on June 16, 1801, John Rogers Vinton was a military man; a scholar in Greek, Latin, and Hebrew and on theology, metaphysics, ethics, and constitutional and international law; and a master of mathematics and fine arts, and his paintings are displayed in many museums and are prized by modern collectors.

Vinton graduated from the West Point Academy and earned a commission at the age of sixteen, making him the youngest lieutenant in history at that time. After proving his merit and military prowess in several key conflicts, and after considering leaving the service to pursue a career of Christian ministry, he fought valiantly in the Battle of Monterey in September 1846. Soon after, he was ordered to join General Scott at the Battle of Vera Cruz, Mexico.

On the evening of March 22, 1847, he had just returned from his post when a large shell hit the top of a parapet, glanced off, and struck him in the head, killing him instantly. The shell did not explode, however, and that very cannonball adorns the top of his grave. After his burial and two days after his death, a letter dated September 23, 1947, arrived at the camp, indicating that he had been promoted to

Top: The box tomb of John Rogers Vinton in Swan Point Cemetery. | Bottom: Hope Memorial Garden.

brevet major "for gallant conduct in the several conflicts at Monterey, Mexico, September 21, 22, and 23, 1846." A large, brown monument was erected in his honor and is easily spotted by the cannonball on top of it.

H. P. LOVECRAFT

Howard Phillips Lovecraft's grave plainly states, "I am Providence," and so he was. A lifelong resident of Providence, the horror-fiction author achieved posthumous fame. During his lifetime his writing was underappreciated, and he died in poverty at the age of forty-six. He is considered one of the greatest authors of the twentieth century, and his settings frequently featured real and fictional New England locations. His books, particularly *The Call of Cthulhu*, have been said to inspire many modern writers, including Peter Stewart, Neil Gaman, and Stephen King.

King has been quoted as saying, "Now that time has given us some perspective on his work, I think it is beyond doubt that H. P. Lovecraft has yet to be surpassed as the twentieth century's greatest practitioner of the classic horror tale."

His stone is arguably the most visited spot in Swan Point Cemetery, even bringing additional visitors as a Pokestop in the *Pokemon Go* game. Visitors leave trinkets of all kinds on the small stone behind the Phillips family obelisk. The small, gray marker can be found at the intersection of Pond Avenue and Avenue B.

COLONEL JOHN S. SLOCUM

Colonel John S. Slocum was a noted abolitionist, attorney, and veteran of the war with Mexico and a leader in the Battle of Bull Run where he was killed. His ornate tomb features a 3-D carving of the American flag, a Civil War–era cap, a uniform, and swords.

BARNABY MONUMENT

The monument to Jerothmul B. Barnaby (1830–1889) is one of the easiest statues to spot in the cemetery. Barnaby was a highly successful dry goods merchant, a Providence City Council member from 1870 to 1879, and a member of the Rhode Island Legislature for one year. Easily the tallest and most recognizable monument in the cemetery, it is in the center at the intersection of the Old Road and Molly Avenue.

HOPE MEMORIAL GARDEN

The Hope Memorial Garden section of the cemetery features plots arranged near an art sculpture made of two large triangular granite pieces with a 1700s-era anchor that was recovered from the nearby Narragansett Bay.

The final resting place of H. P. Lovecraft.

DIRECTIONS

Swan Point Cemetery is located at 585 Blackstone Boulevard in Providence, Rhode Island. Enter the cemetery through the large boulders marking the main gates. Hours are generally 8:00 a.m. to 5:00 p.m. from October through February, and 8:00 a.m. to 7:00 p.m. from April through September. More information may be obtained at www.swanpointcemetery.com.

DeWolfe Cemetery

BRISTOL, RHODE ISLAND

40

SITE HISTORY

Captain James DeWolfe (1764–1837) was a slave trader and privateer during the War of 1812. He was ruthless and was notorious for throwing sick (but still living) slaves into the Atlantic Ocean. He gained notoriety when he was indicted for murdering one of his slaves when the man contracted smallpox. Though his case was later dismissed as "justifiable," in that he was risking the health of other slaves on the property, his fierce reputation was set. He later served in the state legislature and invested in sugar and coffee, making him the richest man in Rhode Island and the second-richest man in the United States.

When DeWolfe retired, he built a large deer park near one of the four family mansions and decided that he liked the area so much that he wanted to make it the final resting place for himself and his wife, Nancy. He commissioned a twenty-foot-high funeral mound and added a decorative iron door to the front of it. He wanted to be able to open the door so his family members could look into the crypt, and reportedly told his children, "As long as any of you are around, you'll see my gold teeth, even when the rest of us is dust."

The final resting place of Captain James DeWolfe.

The crypt was last used in 1925, when George DeWolfe hid from creditors there. Over time, the cemetery grew to include over thirty members of the family. The grave mound is still visible and has a large tree growing straight through the roof of the crypt.

When the captain passed away on Christmas Eve in 1837, followed by his wife a week later, he was not able to rest in peace. On May 11, 1842, under the cover of night and in the middle of a thunderstorm, John Dickinson used gunpowder to blow the door off the crypt to rob the grave—making off with a few gold buttons, an engraved coffin plate, and the captain's gold teeth. The entire lot sold for $6.52, and he paid for the crime on the gallows thirteen years later.

Left and above: Dewolfe Family Cemetery in Bristol, Rhode Island.

DIRECTIONS

The DeWolfe Family Cemetery is located on Woodlawn Avenue in Bristol, Rhode Island. Upon entering the cemetery gate, head straight to the back of the larger right-hand section, and follow the path at the rear of it. Walk a short distance down this path, and the mound will be easily spotted.

ALSO NEARBY

The only surviving mansion belonging to the DeWolfe family is Linden Place, which was featured in the film *The Great Gatsby*, starring Robert Redford and Mia Farrow. Linden Place is located at 500 Hope Street in Bristol, Rhode Island.

Gravelly Point and Goat Island

NEWPORT, RHODE ISLAND

41

SITE HISTORY

Gravelly Point, Rhode Island, is home to a historically "grave" day for pirates. Bull's Point, or Gravelly Point as it was called in the 1700s, is the site of the largest mass public execution of pirates in American history. In June 1723, Newport, Rhode Island, officials had miraculously captured a total of thirty-six men from ships off Block Island and within Newport Harbor. They were rounded up, held, accused of piracy, and tried in court. By July 12, guilty verdicts were handed down, and twenty-six were sentenced to death by hanging. Among the guilty were twenty-five seamen and one ship's captain. The youngest sentenced was seventeen years of age, and the oldest was forty. The hanging took place on July 19, 1723, at the point.

The affair was published far and wide at the time, and many people came from all over New England to witness the event. Among the eager witnesses were some who had suffered injury at the hands of one or more of the pirates and had also attended the court proceedings. For good effect, a Jolly Roger flag was hung alongside them at the gallows.

Goat Island Lighthouse at Newport Harbor, Newport, Rhode Island.

The following twenty-six men (including their ages) were hanged that day:

William Blades, 28	Francis Laughton, 39
John Bright, unknown	Edward Lawson, 20
John Brown, 29	Joseph Libbey, unknown
Charles Church, 21	Thomas Linicar, 21
Peter Cues, 32	Stephen Mundon, 29
Edward Eaton, 38	Thomas Powell, 21
John Fisgerald, 21	William Read, 35
Thomas Hagget, 24	Owen Rice, 27
Charles Harris, 25, ship's captain	Joseph Sound, 28
Thomas Hazel, unknown	James Sprinkly, 28
Daniel Hyde, 23	William Studfield, 40
William Jones, 28	John Tomkins, 21
Abraham Lacy, 21	John Waters, 35

GOAT ISLAND

Goat Island is a small island inside Narragansett Bay and connects to Gravelly Point (also known as Easton's Point) via the Claiborne Pell causeway bridge. The name comes from the fact that the townspeople originally used this island as a goat pasture. The twenty-six pirates hanged at Gravelly Point were buried off the north shore of this island between the tidemarks, as was customary. This watery gravesite, which was originally located along the shoreline, has since been covered by ocean rise and a rock foundation built to fortify a stone fort and lighthouse that now stands at the end of the point.

OUR VISIT

When I visited the Newport Harbor / Goat Island lighthouse, I was surprised to find the grounds set up for a wedding. Rows of white chairs were neatly lined up on what effectively was a group grave. Though it is a beautiful location, and I can see the appeal of being married by the lighthouse, it is akin to holding your ceremony in a cemetery. —S. P.

DIRECTIONS

Goat Island can be reached via Gladys Carr Bolhouse Road off Long Wharf, in Newport, Rhode Island. The Newport Harbor / Goat Island lighthouse is located beside the Hyatt Regency Hotel at 1 Goat Island Road in Newport, Rhode Island.

ALSO NEARBY

Gravelly Point is off Long Wharf and is now referred to as "The Point" or "Easton's Point" after Nicholas Easton, who was a founder of Newport and made his family home at the point. This neighborhood has the highest concentration of colonial homes in New England.

This is because Rhode Island did not follow suit with "industrialization" of their towns and cities as New York and Boston did. Many of the homes are still privately owned and lived in, but a few do offer tours and visiting hours, such as the Hunter House Museum.

You can get a bite to eat at the Rhumbline Bistro at 62 Bridge Street in Newport, which promises an "exquisite dining experience." In seafaring tradition, the term "rhumbline" refers to any of the thirty-two points on a compass and is used in plotting a ship's course. Explore the menu options at www. rhumblinebistro.com.

Houghton Mansion

NORTH ADAMS, MASSACHUSETTS

SITE HISTORY

There is a Massachusetts mansion built in the late nineteenth century that holds a story of tragedy and is also called "home" by a secret society. The Houghton Mansion bears the name of Albert Charles Houghton, a successful businessman who became first the mayor of North Adams, Massachusetts. Mr. Houghton began building the mansion in the 1890s, and he and his wife, Cordelia, and youngest daughter, Mary, moved in toward the end of his term as mayor in 1900. Mr. Houghton continued working at his business following his retirement.

The mansion was a symbol of his wealth and stature in the community. When he reached his sixties, Mr. Houghton's health began failing and his daughter, who loved him dearly and was in her mid-twenties and still living at home, made it her life's focus to care for her weakening father. A tragedy struck one fateful day, August 1, 1914, when there was a horrific automobile accident. The Houghtons had purchased a new, very expensive Pierce-Arrow touring car earlier in the year that their long-time live-in chauffeur, John Widders, had still been learning to drive. The family had decided to go on a pleasure trip to Vermont, and the passengers consisted of Mr. Houghton, daughter Mary, Mary's childhood friend Sybil Cady Hutton, and Sybil's husband, Dr. Robert L. Hutton—and, of course, the driver, John Widders. Mrs. Houghton had chosen to stay home and await their return.

Houghton Mansion, North Adams, Massachusetts.

The quarters of Mary Houghton.

On this morning, the group was traveling up a road now called Oak Hill Road, in Pownal, Vermont, that was undergoing construction. When the car slowly passed a stopped team of workhorses on the left shoulder of the road, it caught some loose dirt and rocks, slipped down an embankment, and flipped over three times before landing in a field at the bottom of the hill. The men all escaped with just minor scrapes and bruises, but the women unfortunately bore the brunt of the disaster. Mary's childhood friend, Sybil, died instantly in the rollover, and Mary herself succumbed to her severe injuries later that afternoon at North Adams Hospital. Mr. Houghton was initially treated in the hospital but was expected to make a complete recovery and was taken home, where a physician and Mrs. Houghton cared for him. Mr. Widders, however, could not deal with the loss of his passengers and the overwhelming pain and guilt of being the driver, and he committed suicide by shooting himself in the head with a horse pistol in a barn on the Houghton property. Soon after, a State of Vermont investigation report blamed the soft shoulder giving way for the accident, which cleared John Widders, and Albert Charles Houghton died at home exactly ten days after the accident.

Following these tragedies, the eldest surviving daughter, Florence Houghton Gallup, and her husband, William A. Gallup, moved into the mansion to take care of Mrs. Houghton until her death less than two years later, in 1916. Florence lived in the home until William retired in 1926, and they decided to move to Boston to be near their son. Florence sold the home to the Freemasons, who still occupy and manage the property today.

Since the Masons took over in 1926, there have been long-standing stories and reports of spiritual presences haunting the mansion. Many paranormal investigative groups, renowned and obscure, have visited the mansion and recorded video and audio evidence of phenomena as well as shared personal experiences. Many believe that the spirits that roam the mansion are Mr. Houghton, Mrs. Houghton, Mary Houghton, and John Widders, as well as other possible persons connected with the property.

The mansion is currently under the care of the Lafayette-Greylock Lodge, which graciously invited us to visit them and experience the mansion for ourselves! They often open the mansion to investigators by appointment, and the public can find special-event dates through their social-media pages.

AUTHOR'S NOTE

I had one of the most profound paranormal experiences I have ever had at the Houghton Mansion. While visiting Mary's bedroom, I was invited to sit in one of her chairs by one of the Masons. He was sensitive to her energy and had been "instructed" to have me sit there. No sooner had I sat back in the chair then I felt a distinct hand on my shoulder. I individually felt each of Mary's fingers curled down onto my shoulder. I'm not ashamed to tell you that I came straight out of that chair, certain that someone had snuck up behind me. It was an experience I will never forget and am eager to replicate. I anxiously await a return visit to this phenomenal home! —S. P.

Our visit to the Houghton Mansion did not disappoint. The mansion exterior is visually very austere and is in need of sprucing up, but this adds all the more to the ambiance. Once inside, entering through the historical side porch entrance, where horse and buggy and later the newly invented Ford automobiles once dropped off family and guests, we saw that the interior was in equal need of upgrade. It was very much original, which was fabulous to see, and enabled us to get into the "feel" of those who walked through the halls and rooms of this grand place.

This property is an especially spiritually supercharged place. We genuinely experienced and interacted with multiple presences, spirits, and intelligent entities within the mansion. There was an especially interesting and "freaky" area where we saw shadow people and did strongly feel a vortex as we walked through the veil where we believe these spirits gather and are able to pass back and forth between their realm and the mansion.

We also interacted with what is thought to be the Houghton daughter as well as past Masonic brothers. There was a great sense of pride and affinity for the brotherly craft relayed by the spirits we encountered in the Masonic temple, which was built as an addition to the main structure of the home. We enjoyed the many interesting stories of the mansion and of their own paranormal experiences as told by members of the Masonic Lodge. Though the Masonic Lodge has recently relocated to another building in South Adams, we very much hope that the current owners will become as respectful caretakers of the property and its history as the Brothers were. —S. G.

The Houghton family plot in South View Cemetery in North Adams, Masschusetts.

DIRECTIONS

The mansion is located at 172 Church Street in North Adams, Massachusetts. This is a neat little town in the upper northwestern corner of Massachusetts, bordering Vermont and New York, and is one of the main towns along the historic and scenic Mohawk Trail (Route 2). The Houghton family plot is located just down the road from the mansion, in Southview Cemetery at 969 Church Street, North Adams.

ALSO VISIT

The Hoosac Tunnel, located nearby, was the second-longest railroad tunnel when it was built from 1851 to 1875. Accidents during the building process killed 193 people, earning the tunnel the nickname "the Bloody Pit." A history of hauntings in the tunnel is documented at www.hoosactunnel.net, and rocks removed from the tunnel area were used to build the wall at the Houghton Mansion property. The tunnel can be accessed at the corner of Whitcomb Hill Road and River Road in Florida, Massachusetts, or through a path in the woods off Church Street, which runs parallel to the railroad tracks close to the intersection of West Shaft Road. A free museum about the Hoosac Tunnel and the railroad industry in general is also available at 115 State Street in North Adams, Massachusetts.

MASSACHUSETTS

43

The *Andrea Gail* Tragedy

GLOUCESTER, MASSACHUSETTS

SITE HISTORY

They that go down to the Sea in ships.

—Psalm 107:23

She's comin' on, boys, and she's comin' on strong.

—Last recorded words of Captain Billy Tyne, October 1991.

October 2016 marked the twenty-fifth anniversary of this tragic tale, which begins and ends on the Atlantic Ocean with a private New England "longliner" fishing vessel named the *Andrea Gail*. She was one in a fleet of twenty based out of Marblehead and Gloucester, Massachusetts. In October 1991, during the height of hurricane season, the *Andrea Gail* was carrying six crew members on its last Grand Banks run and was caught up in the great nor'easter weather event known as "the Halloween Storm" or the more famous "Perfect Storm." The storm itself was a combination of multiple weather systems and was not officially named—thus also being known as the "storm with no name." The vessel was lost at sea somewhere between Sable Island, Nova Scotia, and the Flemish Cap, Newfoundland. The last transmission from the *Andrea Gail* was on October 28, 1991, to Linda Greenlaw onboard the sister ship *Hannah Boden*. The ship was reported overdue on October 30, 1991. An extensive rescue search was launched, and on November 6, 1991, the *Andrea Gail*'s emergency position indicating

The Man at the Wheel Memorial in Gloucester, Massachusetts.

the radio beacon was found washed up on the shore of Sable Island. Later, a few pieces of wreckage were also found, notably the boat's fuel tank and an empty life raft.

Those lost with the *Andrea Gail* were Captain Frank "Billy" Tyne Jr. and crew members Michael "Bugsy" Moran, Dale "Murph" Murphy, Alfred Pierre, Robert "Bobby" Shatford, and David "Sully" Sullivan.

It is surmised that in an effort to get home, the captain and crew braved rough winds and waves, steering straight into this storm system, thinking they could tough it out. What they didn't know was it was not just a storm; it was a convergence of three main storm systems creating a rare monster of massive proportions. At one point, a data buoy's sensor recorded waves between sixty and eighty feet in height (there is discrepancy in the possibility of one-hundred-foot waves purported in other media, which include a book, a movie, and other sources) and a sustained high wind of seventy-five miles per hour, with wind gusts of up to one hundred mph. In the end, the storm endured between October 28 and November 2 and resulted in excess of $200 million in damages spreading along the coastline from Canada to Florida, with New England being the worst hit.

The fateful trip was later immortalized in the creative nonfiction book *The Perfect Storm* by Sebastian Junger. In 2000, the book was made into a blockbuster movie by the same name, starring George Clooney, Mark Wahlberg, John C. Reilly, Diane Lane, and Mary Elizabeth Mastrantonio. The film was nominated for two Academy Awards.

OUR VISIT

The Gloucester Fisherman's Memorial is a beautiful cenotaph designed and erected in 1925 at Gloucester Harbor along Stacy Boulevard in Gloucester, Massachusetts, as a tribute to New England's fishermen. It is listed on the National Register of Historic Places. The rock walls along the esplanade list the names of hundreds of fishermen. Next to this is the Fishermen's Wives Memorial, which was finally built in 2001 after many years of planning and fundraising. The pavers surrounding this monument list many fishermen's family names. It is a beautiful and touching tribute to all who were lost as sea and to their families. Every August, the city of Gloucester holds its annual memorial event. In the end, this story is a reminder to think twice before you decide to flex your muscle to fight against Mother Nature—she will always win.

The Gloucester Fishermen's Memorial

DIRECTIONS

The Gloucester Fishermen's Memorial is located along the esplanade at Stacy Boulevard along the edge of Gloucester Harbor. There is parking immediately along both sides of this street, as well as at nearby shopping areas that are a short walking distance from Stacy Esplanade.

ALSO NEARBY

The much-celebrated local stomping ground of the *Andrea Gail* crew is, of course, the working waterfront pub of choice, The Crow's Nest. They offer pizza and drinks at the horseshoe-shaped bar downstairs, and plain but comfortable and affordable lodging with a harbor view in any one of their fifteen guest rooms upstairs. You can even pick up a hoodie, t-shirt, or ball cap as a souvenir from their small gift shop. The Crow's Nest is located along the waterfront at 334 Main Street, Gloucester, Massachusetts. Visit www.crowsnestgloucester.com.

44

Dogtown Ghost Town

GLOUCESTER, MASSACHUSETTS

SITE HISTORY

Many think that ghost towns are exclusive to the western United States, but New England has its very own seaside ghost town with a rich and colorful history. Dogtown Commons, or Dogtown Village, was a five-square-mile plot of land in Gloucester and Rockport, Massachusetts, which at its peak was home to about one hundred families. Settled in 1693 by residents of Stage Fort Park in Gloucester, the early residents chose the location because it was far enough removed from the coast to give protection from coastal pirates and hostile natives. Dogtown earned its nickname from the many pet dogs that the local women kept for companionship and protection while their husbands were away fighting in the Revolutionary War. After the war, the area became safe again from enemy ships, which led to a revived fishing industry from Gloucester Harbor and new roads being built.

By the end of the War of 1812, most of the local farmers had moved away, and by 1814 only six of the original eighty houses stood. The area became run-down and was something of an embarrassment to locals. Respectable families moved away, and vagrants and criminals looking to lie low moved in. Women without families and war widows stayed behind, and many were accused of witchcraft. Mysterious booming noises, flickering lights, and shadowy figures were observed in the woods, and the locals began to give the area a wide berth.

Tammy Younger, called the "Queen of the Witches," lived on the outskirts of Dogtown on Fox Hill (now known as Cherry Street). Travelers had to pass her door on their way to Dogtown, and she and her aunt Luce George charged a toll to pass. Under the threat of curses and hexes, the passersby were so intimidated they often left corn and fish hoping to curry her favor. Such a fierce reputation

Top: Main entrance to the Dogtown trails.
Below: Site number 15, the former home of Easter Carter

was earned by Younger that when she died in 1829, fear shifted to her spirit. A local cabinetmaker named Hodgkins was commissioned to make her coffin, and his family members were so convinced her spirit was present in their home that they refused to sleep there until she had been buried.

Dorcas Foster lived at 17 Dogtown Road. She had moved to the village as a child when her father was killed during the Revolutionary War. Over her lifetime she was married and widowed three times over. Her last husband, Captain Joseph Smith, fought bravely against the British and was killed in action during the War of 1812.

Isaac Dade was a native Englishman who had been forced to enlist in the British navy. While on a ship bound for Virginia he escaped and eventually fell in love with and married colonist Fanny Brundle. When the pair relocated to Dogtown and the American Revolutionary War commenced, he enlisted in the Continental Army. He fought heroically in the three battles before being badly wounded at the final Battle of Yorktown. He survived, and after witnessing Cornwallis's surrender to George Washington, he returned to his home at 18 Dogtown Road, where he opened a fish store.

Easter Carter, sometimes listed as Esther, lived in the only two-story house in Dogtown. Though it had only a "potato pit" rather than a basement, the pegged clapboard house was quite impressive. Born in England and arriving in the Gloucester area with her brother in 1741, Easter was a spinster who earned a poor and selfless living by nursing those who lived around her. She lived off the land with her cattle, sheep, and team of oxen. Boiled cabbage was her best-known offering to guests, and she was commonly quoted as proclaiming, "Easter Carter eats no trash!"

Easter frequently opened her home to women whom some may have considered undesirable. "Old Ruth," a freed mulatto slave, lived on her second floor. She dressed in male attire and would sometimes go by the name of John Woodman. She was a hard worker and was capable of heavy labor and earned a decent wage building stone walls. Easter even opened her home to two of the reputed witches of Dogtown when their home became too dilapidated for habitation: Becky "Granny" Rich and her daughter, Rachel Smith. Granny Rich told fortunes from coffee grounds and concocted "witch-like brews" from native berries. Rachel assisted her and often created her own "dire drink" by brewing foxberry leaves, spruce tops, and herbs to create a "spring medicine." With their move to Easter's house, it earned a reputation for being a "roadhouse" promoting dancing and frivolity with the youth.

By 1828, the town was mostly abandoned, with many of the dogs left to go feral. The last resident of Dogtown was Cornelius "Black Neil" Finson, who was discovered in 1830 with his feet frozen solid and living in an abandoned cellar hole. He was removed to a Gloucester poorhouse, where he soon died. The final building was razed in 1845, and after a brief period of use by local farmers to graze their animals, it sat in disuse until Roger Babson put the rocky terrain to good use (see page 128). It is currently owned and maintained as biking, hiking, walking, and cross-country skiing trails in perpetuity by the Essex National Heritage Trust.

DIRECTIONS

The trails at Dogtown are most easily reached off Cherry Street in Gloucester, Massachusetts, just past the Sportsman's Club. A parking area is available at the trailhead. It covers 3,600 acres, so taking a map with you is important; maps are readily available online, at the trailhead, and at the Gloucester Office of Tourism at 9 Dale Avenue in Gloucester, telephone 978-282-4101. Several of the former homestead sites have signs complete with QR codes that link to information about that site's history. Visitors are welcome year-round from dawn to dusk, but it should be noted that hunting is permitted in Dogtown October 19–April 1 annually, though never on Sundays, making it the ideal day to go. Daily guided walking tours are available at www.walkthewords.com, by emailing seania@mac.com or by phone at 978-546-8122. The cost is $15 for adults or $8 for children under eighteen. The fee includes complimentary bug repellent, walking sticks, and a "surprise historic snack."

Danvers State Hospital

DANVERS, MASSACHUSETTS

45

SITE HISTORY

Danvers State Hospital for the Criminally Insane was built in 1878 to service Boston-area patients after the nearby asylums in Tewkesbury, Worcester, Taunton, and Northampton became overcrowded. Built during the sanitarium boom of that century, the Gothic-style building was situated on Hathorne Hill, the site of the home of Salem witch trials judge John Hathorne. Made from local bricks and granite, the elaborate structure cost over 1.5 million dollars to construct at a time when much of the country was still recovering from the Civil War.

The impressive structure was said to have inspired H. P. Lovecraft's Arkham Sanitarium in his story "The Thing on the Doorstep," which in turn inspired the Arkham Asylum of Batman fame. Nicknamed the "Castle on the Hill" by locals, it was constructed following the Kirkbride Plan developed by physician and mental health advocate Dr. Thomas Story Kirkbride. The main center building, with its red bricks and many gables and a 130-foot-high central tower, was surrounded by four wings off each side, allowing adequate ventilation and a view of the land surrounding it. Dr. Kirkbride believed that this design could cure patients

The Kirkbride Building of the former Danvers State Hospital.

Danver's State Patient Cemetery. Plots are labeled with numbers only.

and eliminate "the darkest, most cheerless and worst ventilated parts of the hospital." His theory was if you treated the insane well, they would get well.

Over the years, over forty buildings and structures were added to the complex, including a wing for tuberculosis patients, two nursing homes, housing for staff, the Bonner Medical Building, a cemetery, several cottages, and an underground labyrinth of tunnels connecting all these buildings. The patients were treated with positivity and care in a program with a progressive and modern attitude toward the mentally ill. As time went on, however, the patient population ballooned to over 2,000 without an accompanying increase in staff, and by the 1930s the facility was grossly overcrowded and the building was falling into disrepair. Allegations of abuse were rampant, with many claiming that several therapies, including shock and water therapies and prefrontal lobotomies, were being used to subdue patients.

A slow deinstitutionalism started in the 1960s, with many patients moving to community-based group homes or other state hospitals. In 1992, the facility officially closed due to budget cuts and the massive overcrowding. The complex sat empty and crumbling for the next decade. In 2001, filmmaker Brad Anderson chose the abandoned property as the setting and filming location for his thriller *Session 9*. This caused renewed interest in the property, and several preservationist groups attempted to protect it.

In 2005, amid much protesting, the state sold the property to Avalon Bay Development Co., which planned to gut the main building to its facade and build rental apartments inside. Two years later, a massive and unexplained fire seriously delayed progress as much of the new construction burned down. Though the first tenants moved in in 2008, they quickly began to complain of shoddy construction. In 2014, the property changed hands once more and was rechristened Halstead Danvers.

THE CEMETERY

Preservationists recently stumbled across the hospital burial ground in waist-high weeds. The small plot of land was full of stone markers with numbers but no names. They cleaned up the area and erected a cemetery sign declaring the souls of the deceased patients as "the echos [sic] they left behind." Spelling error notwithstanding, the sentiment is a poignant one. They also erected a memorial listing the names of the patients believed to be buried in the yard, and stone benches in front of it create a quiet place for reflection.

A memorial bench has also been placed just inside the entrance, placed in memory of Danvers' "most famous patient," Marie Rose Balter. Ms. Balter was a patient for more than twenty years and later returned to Danvers as chief hospital spokeswoman. Her memoir, *Nobody's Child*, was later turned into a film starring Marlo Thomas, which won a Primetime Emmy and was nominated for two Golden Globes.

AUTHOR'S NOTE

As we drove up to the Kirkbride Building, we both were struck with how visually impressive and oppressive it appears. I had a momentary vision of how it would have felt to be a patient driving up the same path, and I involuntarily shuddered. The thought of living in an apartment that had once housed mentally ill patients undergoing treatment, such as lobotomies, seemed abhorrent, despite how "luxury" they claimed them to be.

As we walked toward the cemetery grounds, a gentleman came out of his garage and waved meekly at us and made a comment on the day's weather. When I asked if he could direct us to the cemetery, he indicated the path we should follow. He remarked that "no one really goes down there," and after a small and slightly dismissive wave to us, he returned inside, and we made our way down the path and entered the grounds.

After shaking our heads and chuckling softly at a misspelling on the cemetery sign, our attitude quickly shifted as we made our way among the unmarked graves—even those that were marked with numbers were still unnamed, and this left us both feeling quite unsettled. We felt as if we were being watched as we read through the many names on the memorial, and we did not feel welcome. Whereas the majority of cemeteries we have visited in the past felt peaceful and inviting, the atmosphere here felt chaotic and uneasy. We didn't think visitors to the grounds were all that common, and as such, our arrival felt intrusive. Perhaps the best solution is to encourage more to stop and pay their respects, and be grateful that advances in the field of psychology have made institutions such as Danvers obsolete. —S. P.

DIRECTIONS

The former Danvers State Hospital for the Criminally Insane is located at 1011 Kirkbride Drive, Danvers, Massachusetts. To access the cemetery, while facing the Kirkbride Building, head right on the sidewalk toward where the apartments end and the condos begin. Behind the first group of condos, follow the path through the field to an opening in the treeline into the cemetery. A more comprehensive history, as well as photos of the property while it housed patients, can be found at www.danversstateinsaneasylum.com .

Danver's State Patient Cemetery.

46

The Boston Strangler

BOSTON, MASSACHUSETTS

SITE HISTORY

In the summer of 1962, women living alone in the city of Boston were gripped with fear as they began to find themselves in the midst of a twenty-month-long killing spree. Sales of new door locks, deadbolts, guard dogs, pepper spray, and other personal-protection items skyrocketed—the Boston Strangler had come to town, and women living alone, regardless of age, race, or socio-economic status, were anything but safe.

Between June 14, 1962, and January 4, 1964, thirteen women were sexually assaulted in their own homes before being brutally murdered, frequently by strangulation with their own household or clothing items. Though there was no set location or age range of the victims, all the crimes were committed without any signs of forced entry, indicating that they either knew their assailant or otherwise allowed his admittance to perform work or make a delivery.

The Boston Strangler took the lives of the following victims during his reign of terror:

Anna Slessers, 55, at 79 Gainsborough Street, Boston—sexually assaulted and strangled with the cord from her house coat. Found 6-14-1962.

Mary Mullen, 85, at 1435 Commonwealth Avenue, Boston —found dead on her sofa after being grabbed and suffering a heart attack. Found 6-28-1962.

Nina Nichols, 68, at 1940 Commonwealth Avenue in Boston —sexually assaulted with a wine bottle and strangled with her silk stockings. Found 6-30-1962.

The murder scene of Anna Slessers, the Boston Strangler's first victim.

Helen Blake, 65, at 73 Newhall Street, Lynn—strangled with her stockings and left face down on her bed. Found 6-30-1962.

Ida Irga, 75, at 7 Grove Street, Boston—sexually assaulted and left with her legs held apart with two chairs and strangled with a pillowcase. Found 8-19-1962.

Jane Sullivan, 67, 435 Columbia Road, Boston—found in her bathtub, kneeling with her bottom exposed. She had been dead for a week and had been strangled by nylon stockings. Found 8-21-1962.

Sophie Clark, 20, at 315 Huntington Avenue, Boston—the hospital technician was found on her back with her legs spread. She had been strangled with an intertwined stocking and petticoat. Found 12-5-1962.

Patricia Bissette, 23, 515 Park Drive, Boston—the receptionist did not arrive for work and was found strangled by four items of her own clothing: a knotted blouse, a nylon stocking, and two other stockings tied together. Found 12-31-1962.

Mary Brown, 69, 319 Park Avenue, Lawrence—found on the floor of her apartment with her head covered with a sheet. She had been strangled, raped, beaten in the head, and stabbed in the breasts with a kitchen fork that had been left in her chest. (The perpetrator, in making his confession, told investigators specifics about Brown's kitchen, including a brass faucet and a yellow radio. When an investigator noted that the sheet must have been bloody, he replied, "Ph, was it, God!") Found 3-6-1963.

Beverly Samans, 23, at 4 University Road, Cambridge—found naked, stretched out on her bed with her hands tied behind her back. She had been stabbed sixteen times (four to the neck and twelve to her chest, including five in her left lung). Two silk stockings were found knotted around her neck, but strangulation was not a primary cause of death. Found 5-6-1963.

Evelyn Corbin, 58, 224 Lafayette Street, Salem—found with two stockings around her neck, a third wrapped around her left ankle, and another on her bed. Found 9-8-1963.

Joann Graff, 23, at 54 Essex Street, Lawrence—found with nylon stockings and a leotard around her neck. Found 11-23-1963.

Mary Sullivan, 19, 44A Charles Street, Boston—her roommates arrived home to find her in her bed and decided to let her sleep. They later tried to rouse her for dinner and discovered her dead, with a nylon stocking and two scarves around her neck. Found 1-4-1964 and becomes the Boston Strangler's final victim.

So who was this mystery killer? The police had little information to go on and got their first lead only while investigating a seemingly unrelated sexual assault. The name Albert DeSalvo would first become known to the general public.

On October 27, 1964, DeSalvo entered a young woman's apartment, posing as a police detective. After tying her up, he raped her before suddenly apologizing and running off. She immediately reported the assault to the police, and her description matched DeSalvo—the man they were investigating as a potential suspect in the "Green Man" (a man who would gain entry to a woman's apartment dressed as a maintenance person in green coveralls before propositioning her for sex) and "the Measuring Man" (where a man would post as a modeling scout and con women into allowing him to take their measurements while groping them) cases. When they released a photo of DeSalvo to the press, women came out of the woodwork to accuse him of similar crimes.

When taken into custody and charged with rape, he allegedly confessed to the thirteen Boston Strangler murders to fellow inmate George Nassar. Nassar then reported the confession to his lawyer, the renowned F. Lee Bailey, who took on DeSalvo's case from that point on. Though he readily repeated his confession to police, and he did know some information that had not been released to the public and would be information only the killer was likely to know,

The murder scene of Evelyn Corbin, the Boston Strangler's eleventh victim.

maximum-security prison in Walpole, Massachusetts. It was at this prison, six years later, that he was found stabbed to death in his cell. Though Robert Wilson of the Whitey Bulger's Winter Hill gang was tried for his murder, his trial ended in a hung jury, and no one was ever held responsible for the crime.

Over the years, doubts about the true identity of the Boston Strangler have been raised. Many have suggested that George Nassar was the true killer. The prison psychiatrist described Nassar as a "misogynistic psychopathic killer" who likely fed details of his crimes to DeSalvo. With DeSalvo named the killer, Nassar could then collect reward money that he would split with DeSalvo's wife and children, and it would feed DeSalvo's internal desire for greater notoriety than being remembered as "the Green Man" and "the Measuring Man." DeSalvo had later recanted his confession, and with his death in prison, it seemed as if the truth had died with him.

However, in 2013, new evidence was discovered in the case of Mary Sullivan, the Boston Strangler's final victim. DNA was successfully retrieved from seminal fluid left beside her body. Officials trailed Tim DeSalvo, Albert's nephew, and retrieved a water bottle that he threw away at a construction site. The DNA produced a familial hit and allowed investigators to pursue a court order to exhume DeSalvo's body from the Puritan Lawn Cemetery in Peabody, Massachusetts. With this direct sample, they were able to definitively link him to Sullivan's murder.

there was no physical evidence that tied him to the crimes. As such, DeSalvo was tried only for the unrelated sexual offenses and some minor robberies and was sentenced to Bridgewater State Hospital for the criminally insane in 1967.

In February of that year, he wrote a letter to the superintendent about the conditions at the institution before escaping with two fellow inmates ,which triggered a massive manhunt. Several days later, he turned himself in and was immediately transferred to the

DIRECTIONS

Albert DeSalvo is buried at Puritan Lawn Memorial Park at 180 Lake Street in Peabody, Massachusetts. It is the oldest memorial park on the East Coast and does not allow traditional gravestones, monuments, or tombs, and only bronze memorials that lie flat on the ground are present. DeSalvo's plot is in Section 5, Lot 374, Grave 2, near the intersection of Cummings Way and Endicott Drive in the rear of the cemetery.

Albert DeSalvo's grave at Puritan Lawn Memorial Park in Peabody, Massachusetts.

47

Salem Witch Hunts

SALEM, MASSACHUSETTS

SITE HISTORY

I am wronged, It is a shameful thing that you should mind these folks that are out of their wits.

—Martha Carrier Hanged, August 19, 1692

In January 1692, nine-year-old Elizabeth Parris and eleven-year-old Abigail Williams began to exhibit strange behaviors. The oceanside town of Salem Village, Massachusetts (now Danvers), was filled with the sounds of their blasphemous screaming, fits, seizures, convulsions, and other odd behavior. Within weeks, several other girls in town also began to go into trancelike states and experience mysterious fits.

The following month, Reverend Samuel Parris, particularly disturbed by his daughter's continued off behavior, called in physicians from across the region to evaluate the girls, but they were unable to find a natural cause. They concluded that the girls were clearly under the influence of Satan.

Extra prayer services and community-wide fasting were ordered by Reverend Parris in hopes of relieving the evil forces inflicting pain on the girls. He began to pressure the girls to reveal the names of the community members responsible for their spells. They hastily named townswomen Sarah Good and Sarah Osborne, as well as Tituba, a Caribbean-born slave in the Parris household.

Though Good and Osborne immediately denied their allegations, Tituba admitted under questioning that she had learned some voodoo practice from her former Barbadian mistress; namely, how to ward herself from evil forces and how to reveal the cause of witchcraft through the baking of "witch cakes." Tituba noted that she had made one containing Elizabeth's urine to try to determine

Top: "The Witch House," home of Justice Jonathan Corwin.
Bottome: The Burying Point in Salem, Massachusetts.

Proctor's Ledge Memorial in Salem, Massachusetts.

VISITING SALEM

Though history has vilified the actions of Hathorne and Corwin, their marks on Salem make fine places to begin a visit. The only structure still standing with direct ties to the witch trials is the home of Jonathan Corwin. Locally referred to as "the Witch House," at the corner of Essex and North Streets, it is maintained as a museum where guests can opt for self-guided tours of the property, with displays of clothing, furniture, and other depictions of life at the time of the trials. It is rumored that Corwin conducted some of his examinations on the property, and though this can't be confirmed, there have been reports of unexplained paranormal occurrences reported by visitors and museum staff.

In 2010, the Gallows Hill Project was created by Elizabeth Peterson, the Director of Corwin's "Witch House," and filmmaker Tom Phillips who brought together a team of experts to re-examine the research Salem historian Sidney Perley carried out in the early twentieth century. They collaborated with Emerson Baker, a Salem State University professor and poured through Perley's research, eyewitness accounts, and historical maps and surmised that the location of the gallows was not in the neighborhood commonly referred to as Gallows Hill, but was actually near the base of Proctor's Ledge. Utilizing the aid of modern technology, including ground-penetrating radar and high tech aerial photography, the team concluded that Proctors Ledge had indeed been the area where so many innocent lives had been taken, and the City of Salem formally recognized and purchased the parcel of land on which the Ledge sits.

On the 325th anniversary of the Trials, Salem Mayor Kim Driscoll dedicated a new memorial in front of a crowd of over 200, including many descendants of the victims. She proclaimed to the crowd "The sun casts few shadows this time of day. Yet the shadows from this site extend across our city in ways we can't see with our eyes". Designed to be a place of reflection for descendants rather than a tourist attraction, it features a semi-circular stone wall that features the names of the 19 victims, each illuminated by a single ground light. In the center of the memorial, a single oak tree has been planted, which Mayor Driscoll called "a symbol of endurance and dignity".

what was afflicting her. She accused others of also participating in witchcraft, especially Sarah Osborne, who Tituba claimed owned a creature with a woman's head, two legs, and wings. She also made confusing statements that the Puritans felt were satanic imagery, including black dogs, hogs, red and black rats and cats, a fox, wolf, and a yellow board. Though others later confessed under duress and coercion, Tituba had the distinction of being the first person in Salem to confess to practicing witchcraft.

In March, the girls set their eyes on a new victim: an upstanding member of the Puritan community, Martha Corey. Her branding as a "witch" meant that Satan's power and reach had extended to even the most pious in the congregation. Suddenly, everyone was fair game, and accusations reached a fever pitch. People of all walks of life found themselves accused, from individuals with prior criminal histories, to others who disturbed puritanical social order, to still-other faithful churchgoers of good standing.

Magistrates John Hathorne and Jonathan Corwin held pre-trial examinations of the accused and heard testimony by "victims," later as members of the Oyer and Terminer Court, and made judgments based on various kinds of evidence, including direct confessions, supernatural attributes such as "witch marks" and owning "familiars," and the controversial "Spectral Evidence," which was based on the assumption that the devil could assume the "specter" of an innocent person to do harm against others.

The Salem Witch Memorial.

The following victims are remembered:

June 10, 1692	Bridget Bishop	Hanged
July 19, 1692	Sarah Wildes	Hanged
July 19, 1692	Elizabeth Howe	Hanged
July 19, 1692	Susannah Martin	Hanged
July 19, 1692	Sarah Good	Hanged
July 19, 1692	Rebecca Nurse	Hanged
August 19, 1692	George Burroughs	Hanged
August 19, 1692	Martha Carrier	Hanged
August 19, 1692	George Jacobs	Hanged
August 19, 1692	John Proctor	Hanged
August 19, 1692	John Willard	Hanged
September 19, 1692	Giles Corey	Pressed to Death
September 22, 1692	Martha Corey	Hanged
September 22, 1692	Mary Easty	Hanged
September 22, 1692	Alice Parker	Hanged
September 22, 1692	Mary Parker	Hanged
September 22, 1692	Samuel Wardwell	Hanged
September 22, 1692	Ann Pudeator	Hanged
September 22, 1692	Margaret Scott	Hanged
September 22, 1692	Wilmot Redd	Hanged

The Burying Point Cemetery on Charter Street is the oldest in Salem, breaking ground in 1637, and is the second-oldest known cemetery in the nation. Centrally located in the small cemetery is the final resting spot of Justice Hathorne. The protective frame surrounding the stone makes it easy to spot when your back is to the lovely old tree in the center of the grounds.

Nearby you will also find the grave of Richard Moore, the "Mayflower Pilgrim," who came across the sea at nine years old as an indentured servant. He rose to the rank of sea captain and died in 1692 at the age of eighty-four, just as the trials were beginning.

A final resting spot is something that many of the victims of the trials were denied because they were prohibited from Christian burials. Rather, just beside the Old Burying Point is the Salem Witch Memorial. The memorial, built and dedicated in 1992 by Maggie Smith and James Cutler following an international competition that garnered 246 entries, features twenty benches cantilevered in a low stone wall, with one for each of the fourteen women and six men who were executed. Each bench is inscribed with the name of the accused, and the date and means of their execution.

Wilmot Redd is further memorialized in nearby Marblehead, Massachusetts. Redd, the wife of fisherman Samuel Redd, was an elderly woman with a reputation for being a bit cantankerous, and she was not especially liked by some of the womenfolk in the village. Captured by Marblehead constable James Smith, Redd was accused of afflicting Eliza Hobert, who claimed her specter threatened to "knock her in the head" if she didn't sign her name in the devil's book, pledging her soul to them.

The trial of Wilmot Redd was particularly dramatic—when she was examined at court on May 31, Mercy Lewis, Mary Walcot, and Abigail Williams fell into fits and claimed her specter was pinching them and commanding them to write in the devil's book. Ann Putnam and Susannah Sheldon also began to writhe about on the courtroom floor but were miraculously cured when Redd was forced to lay her hand upon them. Walcot later affirmed under oath to the Grand Inquest that "she did but look upon me, she would stick me down or almost choke me . . . I believe in my heart that Wilmot Redd is a witch." She was tried and found guilty at the Court of Oyer and Terminer and was hanged on September 22, 1692.

A plaque shaped like a tombstone sits near the eponymously named Redd's Pond in the vicinity of where her house stood "upon the hill by the meet'house" within the Old Burial Hill in Marblehead:

> Old Burial Hill also served as the daytime filming location for the cemetery scenes in the film *Hocus Pocus.*

COPP'S HILL BURYING GROUND

Near the center of Copp's Hill Burying Ground sits a simple stone table memorial dedicating the final resting place of three generations of ministers from the powerful Mather family: Increase, Cotton, and Samuel. Increase Mather (1639–1723) was educated at and was president of Harvard University and was the minister of North Church in Boston. From 1688 to 1692, Mather lived in England and renegotiated the new Massachusetts Charter. In May 1692 he returned with the new Royal Governor

Left: Mather Tomb at Copp's Hill Burying Ground in Boston, Massachusetts.
Right: Wilmot Redd's stone at Old Burial Hill Cemetery in Marblehead, Massachusetts.

William Phips to find the colony in the full grip of witch trial hysteria.

Though he was at times publicly critical of the proceedings, he was also present at the trial of George Burroughs, and he felt his execution "just." His unease with the trials, especially the court's decision to admit Spectral Evidence, grew, and in October 1692 he addressed his concerns to a convocation of local ministers. This speech was later published as "Cases of Conscience concerning Evil Spirits Personating Men," along with a letter written by royal elite member Thomas Brattle to English clergymen, which concluded, "I am afraid that ages will not wear off that approach, and those stains, which these things will leave behind them up on our land." In October of that year, the colonial governor dissolved the local Court of Inquiry, and the convictions and executions came to an end.

LOCATIONS

Salem Pioneer Village, 1630—Forest River Park, Salem

Witch House—310½ Essex Street, Salem

Proctor's Ledge Memorial—Pope Street, Salem

Burying Point Cemetery—Charter Street, Salem

Salem Witch Trials Memorial—beside Burying Point Cemetery, Salem

Redd Pond—Old Burial Hill, Pond Street, Marblehead

Mather Tomb—Copp's Hill Burying Ground, intersection of Hull and Snowhill Streets in Boston

ALSO VISIT

House of the Seven Gables, the inspiration for Nathaniel Hawthorne's novel; Hawthorne was a lifelong Salem resident and the great-great-grandson of Judge John Hathorne. He was so embarrassed by his connection to the tragic history of his hometown that he added the "w" to his surname. Visit the House of Seven Gables at 115 Derby Street, Salem, Massachusetts.

MASSACHUSETTS

48

New England Pirate Museum and Pirates of Boston

SALEM AND BOSTON, MASSACHUSETTS

SITE HISTORY

Yes, I do heartily repent. I repent I had not done more mischief; and that we did not cut the throats of them that took us, and I am extremely sorry that you aren't hanged as well as we.

—Anonymous pirate, asked on the gallows if he repented

JOE BRODISH

Joe Brodish made a fortune for himself and his pirate crew by attacking and capturing Spanish ships. Upon returning to New England, he was recognized and arrested for his pirate activities. After Brodish escaped from the Boston jail, not once but twice, it was discovered that the jail keeper was his uncle. Brodish was shipped off to England and hanged.

WILLIAM FLY

William Fly was a boatswain aboard a slave ship. He led a mutiny, killed the captain, renamed the ship *Fame's Revenge*, and became a pirate chief. Known for his cursing rages and inhuman brutality, Fly often whipped his captives for up to one hundred lashes. He pirated many vessels along the New England coast and was finally captured off the coast of Newburyport and brought to Boston for execution. He went to his execution with a nosegay in his hand and reproached the hangman for not knowing his craft

Murals along the side of the New England Pirate Museum.

as he fixed the noose around his own neck with his own two hands. Fly was gibbeted at Nix's Mate Island in Boston Harbor. His pirate career had lasted only one month.

JACK QUELCH

Jack Quelch was the chosen commander of the *Charles* after its captain had been dumped overboard at Half Way Rock outside Salem Harbor. Quelch led the crew in pirate raids off the coast of South America, and upon returning to Marblehead, he and many of his crew were arrested. He was hanged in Boston in 1704.

THOMAS TEW

Thomas Tew, also known as the "Rhode Island Pirate," flourished actively in piracy in Rhode Island in the late 1690s. This pirate's legacy is created from partial truths and fiction, since there is very little official information that can be confirmed on early details, including his connections to pirate lore, due to scant records kept for that period of time. It is speculated that Thomas was born either in Rhode Island or within the colonies to English parents and ended up in Rhode Island, or possibly immigrated there from England as a child with his family.

It is known that as an adult Thomas Tew became a licensed privateersman but quickly turned to piracy. His initial pirate cruise took place in Bermuda, where he was commissioned by government supporters there and given a sloop named the *Amity* to take down a French operation in the Republic of Gambia off the coast of West Africa. Captain Tew did not carry out his commissioned task, because it was during this sail that he requested his crew to join him in taking up piracy, to which they heartily agreed. In 1693 they entered the Red Sea and proceeded to plunder Arabian and Indian cargoes. Captain Tew had eagerly urged his crew to continue the robbery of convoys throughout the Indian Sea, but the idea was opposed by his quartermaster and he stood down.

Tew's illegal pirate activity caused much disapproval and disruption back in the New England colonies as well as in Europe, as Governor Benjamin Fletcher of New York (served 1692–1697) was fired by Edward Randolph, the Crown's agent overseeing

The site of the Great Elm Tree and the gallows on Boston Common.

trade, for being too friendly with Captain Tew and enabling the harbor of pirates in the Province of New York (1664–1776). To prevent action against Captain Tew, Governor Fletcher had paid off the owners of the *Amity* upon Tew's return with a hoard worth approximately fourteen times more than the vessel!

Despite England's official opposition to piracy, the governor approved a new letter of marque for Tew, and he set sail back to the Red Sea. With each stop along the journey to the Red Sea, Tew's crew increased. He also befriended other pirate captains along the way and even came across Henry Avery sailing aboard the armed warship the *Fancy*. Tew and these pirate captains all decided to sail forward in concert. During this time, in June 1695, Tew and his pirate convoy pursued and attacked a Mughal Empire ship passing through the Mandab Strait, and Tew was killed in this battle. Unaware of Tew's death, King William III commissioned William Kidd, before he turned pirate, with the search and capture of Thomas Tew.

Tew's final resting place is not known, but as mentioned previously, his continued legacy is the stories of his possible connections to Ratsimilao, a man who created a kingdom called "Betsimisakara" spreading out along 400 miles of the East Coast region of Madagascar, including the island's largest bay, and to the supposed pirate colony of "Libertatia," also said to be located somewhere in the coastal regions off Madagascar.

THE WOMEN OF PIRACY

There were a few hardy women who also enjoyed a pirate life! Most of them were from English or European descent and either were wives of pirate captains or were born into a nautical family. The most-famous female pirates were Anne Bonny and Mary Reid, each of whom has a brave story behind her. There is but one officially documented female pirate of New England.

Rachel Wall (née Schmidt) was born in the colony of Pennsylvania around 1760, and when she came of age made her way to Boston Harbor, where she met her fisherman husband, George Wall. She had officially sailed as a pirate with her husband and a small crew, duping and sometimes murdering innocent bystanders in and around the Isles of Shoals (Maine and New Hampshire) area for only one year, from 1781 to 1782, but she is notorious within New England on a few points. Her piratical activity was short lived and confined to the Isles of Shoals and Boston Harbor. She may well have been the first North American–born female to be documented as a pirate, and in the year 1789 she was the very last woman to be hanged in the colony of Massachusetts. She was hanged for robbery on Boston Common but made it known at her execution that she did indeed prefer to be known and die as a pirate, although maintaining a claim of innocence regarding the accusation of murder and highway robbery.

Blackbeard statue outside of the New England Pirate Museum in Salem.

DIRECTIONS

The New England Pirate Museum is located at 274 Derby Street in Salem, Massachusetts. Hours vary by season and should be confirmed by visiting www.piratemuseum.com. The museum not only features displays about sixty buccaneers who roamed the New England coast but also includes a re-created dockside village, a pirate ship, and an eighty-foot bat cave filled with "hidden bootie," all of which you can visit. Discounts are available for visitors who also want to explore the museums related to Salem's witch trial history.

The site of the Great Elm, where many pirates and other criminals met their demise at the gallows, is on Boston Common. Though the tree was removed after it was heavily damaged in a gale in 1876, a plaque was installed where it stood. It is located not far from the Frog Pond. Boston Common is located at the corner of Tremont and Park Streets in Boston, Massachusetts.

49

Dungeon Rock

LYNN, MASSACHUSETTS

Dungeon Rock in Lynn Woods, Lynn, Massachussetts.

SITE HISTORY

Lynn Woods is located inside the coastal city of Lynn, Massachusetts. It has two bays that make up its beaches: Nahant Bay and Broad Sound. This area was frequented by pirates in the 1500s–1700s. Dark pirate ships, sometimes displaying a sinister all-black flag as a warning, were seen lurking off this coast many times during the golden age of piracy. Thomas Veal is arguably one of the most notable out of a handful of pirates known to come ashore from their ships and seek refuge in these woods. When Massachusetts authorities got word that one such ship was Pirate Veal's, they proceeded to approach the ship in hopes of detaining him.

Veal avoided capture by hiding in a natural cave in Lynn Woods called Dungeon Rock. He reportedly hauled and hid his load of treasure there. He was able to call the cave at Dungeon Rock home for quite some time until an earthquake, of all things, shook the area and knocked down a huge piece of boulder onto the cave entrance and sealed it for good. Legend has it that Thomas Veal may have been inside at the time and was either crushed to death or trapped along with his pirate booty. It is widely believed that Pirate Veal's remains have been locked inside this cave for at least 200 years.

Beginning in the 1830s, there were multiple attempts to blast open the rocks to reveal the cave and search for Veal and his treasure. All were unsuccessful. In 1852, Hiram Marble, a devoutly religious man, came to the cave stating that he had received spiritual messages from the ghost of Thomas Veal, which requested that he go to Dungeon Rock and search for the treasure. Hiram tried for many years, putting immense money, labor, and time into the endeavor, and even passed on the mission to his son, Edwin, who became so consumed by this search that he requested to be buried atop Dungeon Rock when he passed away. His final resting place is marked by a large pink boulder just outside the entrance to the cave.

To this day, Veal's treasure has never been found, but his spirit is thought to continue the search in the afterlife.

Dungeon Rock has a "Pirate Day" held annually in October. It's a celebration about kids, pirates, and fun during the fall foliage season. The Hog's Breath Inn offers pirate grub at in relation to this event. It's a jolly good time for young and old! More-detailed information about Lynn Woods can be found at www.lynnwoods.org.

Dungeon Rock.

a.m. and bolted shut at 2:30 p.m. daily. It is a short walk down some wooden stairs to begin the cave self-tour through some very dark, cold, and wet underground passages. Be prepared with good flashlights, a jacket or sweatshirt, and steady shoes! You may also get the creepy feeling of being watched as you pass over the bridge. Yes, there is a bridge down there . . . and we believe there is something else lurking in the cavern darkness. There were footsteps heard behind us (there was no one else touring at the time), and both of our two young companions (our ten-year-old sons) saw an upper torso and face of a man waving to them as it made a ghostly appearance out of the darkness. This was accompanied by all of our flashlights, cameras, and cell phones malfunctioning and the absolute feeling that someone was present and watching us. When we returned aboveground, the flashlights and cameras worked fine without interruption. —S. G.

AUTHOR'S NOTE

The Lynn Woods Reservation is a wonderful 2,200-acre forest park located in the city of Lynn, Massachusetts. It's a beautiful area for walking, hiking, picnicking, and exploration. Most areas of the woods are pet and child friendly and include many interesting and curious sites, such as Dungeon Rock, the Rose Garden, the Wolf Pits, Stone Tower, Walden Pond, Birch Pond, Breed's Pond, and many rocky, mountainous, and swampy areas of terrain.

It is a bit of a hike over trails and up steep, rocky steps to the final cave opening of Dungeon Rock. At the top of these huge boulders is the pink boulder that marks the burial place of Edwin Marble, the son of one of the excavators of Dungeon Rock who also worked to find Pirate Veal's treasure. The entrance and exit to the cave are protected by ominous heavy iron doors, which are opened at 9:00

DIRECTIONS

Dungeon Rock is located in the Lynn Woods Reservation, the second-largest municipal park in the United States, on Pennybrook Road in Lynn, Massachusetts. Upon arriving at the main entrance to Lynn Woods, you will see parking near a picnic area and basketball court. Start your hike by taking Jackson Path and follow the trail to Dungeon Rock. Hint: if you see picnic tables and an iron-fenced area to your right as you walk, you are headed in the right direction! There are also handy park maps available at the entrance area.

ALSO NEARBY

An excellent meal of Angus burgers, steak tip salads with house-made dressings, and lemonade can be had at the Four Winds Pub and Grill at 265 Broadway, along the banks of Sluice Pond in Lynn. The local favorite has been open since 1939 and features impressive views with weekly live music and first-responder specials. The menu and entertainment schedule can be viewed at www.fourwindspub.com.

Longfellow's Wayside Inn

SUDBURY, MASSACHUSETTS

50

SITE HISTORY

One Autumn night, in Sudbury town,
Across the meadows bare and brown,
The windows of the wayside inn
Gleamed red with fire-light through the leaves
Of woodbine, hanging from the eaves
Their crimson curtains rent and thin.

And, half effaced by rain and shine,
The Red Horse prances on the sign.
Round this old-fashioned, quaint abode
Deep silence reigned, save when a gust
Went rushing down the county road,
And skeletons of leaves, and dust,
A moment quickened by its breath,
Shuddered and danced their dance of death,
And through the ancient oaks o'erhead
Mysterious voices moaned and fled.

—Henry Wadsworth Longfellow

Tales of a Wayside Inn

HISTORY

In Boston's MetroWest town of Sudbury, Massachusetts, sits a charming throwback of colonial charm. What began as a humble and modest private home in 1702 became America's first inn in 1716, and later, thanks to Henry Wadsworth Longfellow, it earned a spot in literary history.

Top: Longfellow's Wayside Inn in Sudbury, Massachusetts.
Bottom: The historic Room 9.

MASSACHUSETTS

In 1702, local landowner David Howe built a two-room homestead along the Old Boston Post Road for his pregnant wife, Hepzibah Death. When he realized how many travelers passed his doorstep on a daily basis along the main coach travel and mail route from Boston, Worcester, and New York, he applied for a licence to open a "house of entertainment," known as the Red Horse Tavern. Immediately after completing an addition to the house, travelers and lodgers made the Howes the first innkeepers in the nation.

The inn passed down from Howe father to son (from David to Colonel Ezekiel to Adam to Lyman), each adding on to the inn's size: between 1750 and 1760 adding a total of eight guest rooms and a new gambrel-style roof, constructing a new kitchen in 1785, and later building a large kitchen with two chambers above it (now rooms 9 and 10).

When Lyman died unmarried at the age of sixty in 1861, the inn was inherited by relatives who were largely disinterested in continuing to run the property as a full-scale inn. They did rent out the hall for weddings and dances and occasionally longer residential stays. In November of that year, an auction was held to settle $6,000 in debts, including the sale of many Howe family heirlooms.

The year following Lyman's death, the old Howe Tavern and Red Horse Inn was visited by noted poet Henry Wadsworth Longfellow and his publisher, James Fields. It was a visit that would gain the inn its literary significance. Longfellow selected the tavern as the setting for his characters in 1863's *Tales of a Wayside Inn*. Due to the book's immense popularity, selling out completely on the first day of its release, the inn became a haven for day-trippers seeking to visit the tavern captured in its stories. Years before any official change, local merchants began selling souvenirs referring to the old Howe property as Longfellow's Wayside Inn, and the name was formally changed to such in 1897.

It was this literary connection that brought about the most significant period of development on the property. Due in large part to his fondness for Longfellow's poetry, automobile industrialist tycoon Henry Ford purchased the Inn in 1923, with the goal of transforming it into a living-history museum. Ford purchased 3,000 acres of property around the inn, added eight buildings to

The front of the gristmill at Wayside Inn.

the grounds, and repurchased, returned, and displayed many items sold in the 1861 auction.

In addition to having a fully operational gristmill installed, which furnished flour both for the inn and King Arthur Flour and Pepperidge Farm, Ford had the Redstone School built, the one-room schoolhouse reputed to be the schoolhouse in Sarah Josepha Hale's famous poem "Mary Had a Little Lamb." He also opened the Wayside Inn School for Boys to train local indigent boys for work in his Michigan factories. It was boys from the school who built the nondenominational Martha-Mary Chapel, named after Ford's mother and mother-in-law, using trees from the property that had toppled during a hurricane in 1938.

The inn benefited from Ford's notoriety and stature, and it gained an international reputation, drawing notable visitors including President Calvin Coolidge and Charles Lindbergh. Unfortunately, in December 1955, a devastating fire ravaged much of the inn, and the board of directors, who included several members of the Ford family, quickly stepped in to exact the necessary renovations—but it came at a significant cost. The family transitioned management of the inn to the National Trust for Historic Preservation, a charitable foundation, for a short period of time before control was passed on to a board of trustees, which led to its current self-sustainability. The Wayside Inn Historic District earned local historic-district designation in 1967 and state historic-landmark status in 1970 and became a National Register Historic District in 1973. It celebrated its 300th anniversary in 2016.

HAUNTS FROM HISTORY

Today's modern visitors come to the property for many reasons, not only as fans of Longfellow or colonial history but also as paranormal aficionados.

Reports of hauntings at the inn date back to 1868, as recorded in the Inn Hostess' journal. In the inn's archive are notes, written in the hostess's own handwriting, about an incident where she saw a ghost "half floating and half running" through the room now known as the Hobgoblin Room.

The Wayside Inn's most famous spirit is that of Jerusha Howe, Lyman's sister. She was far from the typical country girl of that area and time period. According to *Harper's New Monthly Magazine*, Jerusha "possessed great common sense, combined with refined tastes, musical accomplishments, and rare domestic abilities. She was delicate in person, not of robust constitution, which kept her much at home under the care of watchful parents."

Miss Jerusha, also referred to as "'The Belle of Sudbury,' owned the only piano in town, and was known to play 'The Battle of Prague' and 'The Copenhagen Waltz' and sang with a 'thin and decorous voice.'"

She was much sought after by the men of Sudbury, but her heart was taken by a visitor from England who had taken up residence in the inn. When he was suddenly called back to England, he vowed to return and marry her but never did so. Though it is unknown if he was lost at sea or had a betrothed in England, it is well known that Jerusha's heart never recovered. She rejected all future suitors and died alone and unmarried at age forty-five in 1842.

The ghost of Jerusha reportedly never left rooms 9 and 10, which she occupied in life. In the rooms, which look now as they did then, guests report being awakened by the sensation of a soft breath on their face, only to open their eyes to be looking into Jerusha's eyes before she fades away; they also report soft touches and caresses and the sensation of someone slipping into the bed and snuggling up with them. There have often been reports of a cool breeze wooshing past guests and employees up the back stairway leading to her room, and the smell of her usual citrus perfume all over the inn. When the inn is quiet, employees have heard her piano, which is preserved behind glass on the main floor, playing "The Copenhagen Waltz." The level of paranormal activity is so frequent that employees openly share their experiences; it is noted on the inn's website and on paranormal television programs such as *Ghost Adventures* that have filmed at the property.

SECRET DRAWER SOCIETY

In the 1950s, the then innkeeper Frances Koppels started a new tradition that persists to this day. He told the visiting children to hunt for hidden drawers in their rooms. In camouflaged panels in walls and furniture, Koppels hid small toys and candy. Over time guests began leaving their own notes and treats. In room 9, they are found not only in the furniture, but in the ceiling beams and even in a compartment full of "hidden treasure." These mementoes are taken from and added to by anyone lucky enough to find them, but to preserve the fun, we won't give you any hints to their location!

The first mixed drink in the nation, the Coow Woow, concocted of rum and ginger brandy, was made at the Red Horse Tavern and is still available to the daring. It is quite strong!

AUTHOR'S NOTE

Though I had visited the inn several times and spent the night in one of the more modern rooms, I had been eager to return to stay in one of the historical rooms, either room 9 or 10. I eagerly called and crossed my fingers that we would be able to secure a night in room 9. The friendly woman who answered the phone remembered my name from a previous visit (the benefit/curse of a unique name!) and wished me luck, suggesting her next available weekend night for several months ahead. No dice with our schedules. After a few more misses, we were able to lock down an evening in June of the 300th-anniversary year, and I began a countdown akin to a child at Christmas!

With our full selection of paranormal investigation gear at the ready, we loaded into room 9 and hoped to make contact with Miss Jerusha Howe. We set up our night vision cameras and DVR system and immediately began seeing orbs fly across the screen. We decided to leave the cameras running and make our way down to the dining rooms. When we returned, we stopped by a display of Howe family personal items, and we came upon a small room beside our room's back door.

While we were commenting on the beauty of a collection of Jerusha's fans, Sandra began to feel light taps and gentle brushes against her back, but there was no one behind her. She suddenly felt a tug on her left elbow and asked, "Was that you?" I replied, "Was what me?," and I assured her that I had not touched her and was standing too far away from her to have done so inadvertently. Since we were within feet of our room, and knowing that these were similar behaviors to what hundreds of other guests have experienced, we wondered if someone was trying to make contact, and we quickly returned to our room eager to begin investigating.

After an unsuccessful electromagnetic field (EMF) sweep and EVP session, we began a pendulum session using a mat with answering text and began to get what appeared to be intelligent responses to questions we posed. It was getting quite late, and after problem-solving an issue—we tried to keep the camera we'd initially positioned outside the bathroom (which didn't seem to be acceptable to the spirits, since it worked well anywhere else in the room)—we called it a night and let the cameras continue to run as we slept.

While I have admittedly had difficulty sleeping in other haunted locations (see my note on the Lizzie Borden Bed and Breakfast), my evening's rest in room 9 was deep and refreshing! When dawn woke us, we both had been surprised and assumed that the spirits of the inn had decided not to visit with us. We went downstairs for a breakfast that was as equally delicious as our previous night's dinner. After dismantling our camera system, we said our goodbyes and made plans to return again to further try our luck.

It was only after reviewing the footage at home that we noticed, in addition to many, many orbs at 2:51 and 3:03 in the morning, the blanket at the foot of the bed a few feet below my feet was jerked. Despite viewing the occurrence from multiple camera angles, we were unable to find an explainable reason for the movement, such as the movement of my legs. At no other point in the seven-plus hours we slept did the blankets move again. Was it Jerusha trying to get our attention? View the footage for yourself at our YouTube channel "ScaryNewEngland" and tell us what you think is occurring! —S. P.

The front of the Martha-Mary Chapel.

DIRECTIONS

Longfellow's Wayside Inn is located at 72 Wayside Inn Road in Sudbury, Massachusetts. Reservations for lodging, dining, and special events can be made by dialing 978-443-1776 or by visiting their site online at www.wayside.org.

51

Rutland Prison Camp

RUTLAND, MASSACHUSETTS

SITE HISTORY

Within Rutland State Park in Rutland, Massachusetts, lies the remnants of a former prison camp. The camp was established in 1903 by the General Court of Massachusetts as an industrial camp for low-level criminal offenders, mostly drunkards serving short-term sentences. The prison featured dormitories for prisoners, homes and cottages for staff, and a fully functioning 150-acre farm. The farm grew potatoes, which were shipped to the large state prison, and raised chickens and sixty purebred Holstein cows. Production at the farm was so successful that they were able to provide for all the prison needs as well as annually selling $11,000 in eggs and $5,000 in milk to the nearby city of Worcester.

When a tuberculosis outbreak occurred at the prison camp in 1907, a hospital with thirty beds was quickly built. The prison remained in use until 1934, when it was discovered that the grounds were built on a watershed drainage area for the Ware River that was flowing into the newly built Quabbin Reservoir, which supplied drinking water to Boston. The land and buildings were sold to the Metropolitan District Water Supply Commission, and several of the buildings remain covered in graffiti and are slowly crumbling today.

The most prominent of the remaining structures is a large root cellar against the forest edge. The large stone doorway leads to a cavernous area originally used to store the farm's products prior to their use or sale. Now the area is heavily graffitied and shows other evidence of vandalism, including the setting of fires and, ironically, the broken bottles abandoned by partyers.

Solitary Confinement cells at Rutland Prison Camp, Rutland, Massachusetts.

To the right of the root cellar is the wide-open field that served as the recreation yard. Directly across from this place of freedom was the spot of most restriction: the solitary-confinement cells. These six small cells were the prison camp's most intensive means of behavior modification, with New England weather in winter and summer making the cell temperatures difficult to withstand.

The property is often descried by visitors as having a foreboding or spooky air to it. It is not just the visions of bygone prisoners or vandalized buildings that make visitors feel creeped out. The property has long been visited by paranormal enthusiasts, and many experienced ghost hunters have reported experiencing disembodied voices, full-bodied apparitions of prisoners and guards, and the sounds and sensations of being followed.

Local author Jodi Mayhan detailed her experiences investigating the prison grounds in her 2013 book, *The Soul Collector*. Mayhan had investigated the property in a depressed state following a relationship breakup, and a negative entity attached itself to her and followed her home. One of her friends was a psychic medium and told her that she had encountered the spirit at the tuberculosis hospital and that it had hundreds of spirits lined up behind "him." He was determined to take her soul as well, and it took considerable work over a six-month period for Mayhan to release his influence. She wrote the book as a cautionary tale for other investigators on how to avoid attachments.

AUTHOR'S NOTES

Driving into the prison camp area via the long dirt road, although deep in the woods, is not intimidating during the day, but it can turn pretty creepy at nightfall. The solitary-confinement buildings were small, cramped, and uncomfortable looking, and I didn't care to walk inside any of the cells but didn't really feel any strong vibes around them, either. The root cellar, however, is what really felt unnerving, and it appeared to hold both a lot of residual and intelligent energy. Summer had been to the property previously and noted that there was a distinct shift in vibe on this day—describing it as "off."

We both had very strong feelings of not being welcome there and felt the boundary at the opening of the root cellar to be very occupied and presenting some strong pushback when we were trying to film, photograph, and investigate. We were not able to

walk to the rear of the root cellar, and Summer vocalized feeling creeped out, and I had the strange, though not exactly threatening, sense of being held back from stepping farther into the opening as I filmed. Summer paused taking photographs to start a ghost box session, and we quickly started hearing some negative phrases such as "kill" and "hurt you," and she reminded me of the adage "when in doubt, get out." As we turned and walked back to the car, we immediately heard heavy footsteps rapidly following behind us, and we felt urgency in needing to leave the area quickly. When I got to the driver's side of the vehicle, got in, and shut the door, I distinctly felt a presence at the door looking into the driver's side window with the angry message of "leave now!," and Summer had confirmed that feeling. I definitely knew we needed to go at that time! It was only later as we reviewed our photos from this location we discovered an orb in one single shot that, when zoomed in on, appeared to show an angry screaming face. Pareidolia or not, it certainly left an impression on both of us. —S. G.

Right: The root cellar at Rutland Prison Camp.
Left: "Face" within the orb.

DIRECTIONS

Rutland Prison Camp is located on Prison Camp Road, Rutland, Massachusetts. Drive straight when you enter at the main State Park entrance down a long dirt road. The buildings are easily accessible, and you can drive right up to the root cellar. Access to the prison camp and nearby hiking trails is free, but a fee is charged to enter the lakeside beach area for swimming, boating, and picnicking.

ALSO VISIT

The Rutland Prison Camp cemetery is located behind the Goose Hill Cemetery on Charnock Hill Road in Rutland. Follow the small trail at the rear of Goose Hill Cemetery, and you will find a marker where crosses once marked the graves of the fifty-nine inmates buried there.

Granary Burying Ground

BOSTON, MASSACHUSETTS

52

SITE HISTORY

The Revolutionary War, the Freedom Trail, the Boston Massacre, Redcoats, old meetinghouses, and the Midnight Ride are just a few of the things that may come to mind when you think of historic Boston. There is a spot nestled in-between tall city buildings and residential walk-ups where many of Boston's heroes and New England's influential American patriots rest in peace within the city they loved and fought for: Granary Burying Ground. Named for the 12,000-bushel grain storage that was once adjacent to the land, historical notables you can find here include signers of the Declaration of Independence such as Robert Treat Paine, John Hancock, and Samuel Adams; the great Paul Revere; and Peter Fanueil, the colonial merchant and slave trader who donated the notable landmark Fanueil Hall to the city of Boston. Many Boston mayors, individuals associated with the Salem Witch Trials, members of Benjamin Franklin's family, Phillis Wheatley (the first African American woman to publish a book), and even a woman believed to be the author of the children's nursery rhyme "Mother Goose" are buried within the confines of the Burying Ground.

There are also "common" graves in which more than one person was laid to rest, such as the African American victim of the Boston Massacre, Crispus Attucks, and at least four other victims of the massacre. An Infant's Tomb, which holds the remains of nearly 1,000 young souls sits toward the center of the grounds. The oldest grave markers date to 1667, and this site, like other cemeteries of the period, holds hundreds or even thousands of

Granary Burying Ground, Boston, Massachusetts.
Bottom right: The final resting place of John Hancock.

nameless bodies in shared graves without markers in layers beneath the topsoil. The burial ground was built in 1660, when King's Chapel Cemetery and six other major burying grounds were rapidly filling up and were deemed not sufficient to hold the city's dead due to an ever-increasing population; it now contains 2,300 markers for over 5,000 Bostonians.

We are reminded by this site, along with many others of Revolutionary War significance, that not all that is historical is aboveground. In 2009, a tourist accidentally found what turned out to be an old stairway to an underground crypt when she tripped and fell hip deep into sunken ground near Paul Revere's grave marker! Talk about discovering history! There are thousands of souls that lie buried and undisturbed in the hallowed grounds of Boston.

AUTHOR'S NOTE

The Granary Burying Ground is one of six major burial grounds in Boston. Like each of these, it has strict hours of operation between 9:00 a.m. and 5:00 p.m. year-round, and due to its downtown location, parking is extremely scarce. The surrounding establishments do not have public restrooms unless you are a paying patron, so plan accordingly. —S. G.

Main gate to Granary Burying Ground.

DIRECTIONS

Granary Burying Ground is located on Tremont Street in downtown Boston, Massachusetts.

ALSO NEARBY

The Freedom Trail is a 2.5-mile red-lined route through sixteen historic sites, including historic meetinghouses, burying grounds, and Paul Revere's home, from which he famously departed for his Midnight Ride. Join an organized tour or follow the line independently with a smartphone app or a map downloaded from www.thefreedomtrail.org. Some sites charge small admission fees.

Ziggy's Coffee Bar is directly across the street from the burying-ground entrance at 102 Tremont Street. The very friendly staff provides quick service and excellent coffee, tea, and pastries. They also offer some alcoholic brunch cocktail options, including Ziggy's Espresso Martinis, the "Screwmosa" (a screwdriver meets a mimosa), and house-made sangria. For a complete menu of their offerings, visit www.ziggyscoffeebar.com.

53

Roger Babson

GLOUCESTER AND WELLESLEY, MASSACHUSETTS

SITE HISTORY

It takes a person who is wide awake to make his dream come true.

—Roger Babson

Roger Babson (1875–1967) was a Massachusetts-born entrepreneur, businessman, economist, writer, and philanthropist. A member of the tenth consecutive generation to be born and live their lives in the Gloucester area, he joined a long lineage of prominent citizens, including sea captains and preachers, and he felt a strong connection both to Protestantism and the skills, traits, and attributes of the Forefathers.

In 1919, Babson founded Babson College, a private business school with a focus on entrepreneurship education in nearby Wellesley, Massachusetts, and began a series of writings, including his much-heralded *Ten Commandments of Investing*, and he published over forty books on economics and social problems.

During the Great Depression in the 1930s, Babson became interested in the history of the abandoned settlement of Dogtown in his native Gloucester. To provide charitable assistance to local unemployed stonecutters, he commissioned them to carve inspirational sayings on approximately two-dozen boulders surrounding the Dogtown area. Some of the inscriptions include "Help Mother," "Get a Job," "Spiritual Power," "Keep out of Debt,"

Top: Babson Boulder encouraging you to "Help Mother."
Bottom: The graves of Roger, Grace, and Nona Babson.

and "Loyalty." Popular hiking trails wind through the area, with many of the boulders clearly visible on or just off the main trails, referred to as the Babson Boulder Trail.

For two years (1936–1938), Babson served as a national church moderator for the General Council on the Congregational Christian Churches. After ostracizing fellow members for espousing a belief that it was a shift in the general society toward becoming morally corrupt that was resulting in an overall decline in church attendance, he left the council. He soon became involved in the Open Church movement, in which places of worship have open doors at all hours of the day and night, every day of the year, and in 1938 he founded the national offices of the Open Church Association in Gloucester.

In 1940, Babson ran for president of the United States as the candidate for the Prohibition Party. Though he ultimately lost to incumbent president Franklin Delano Roosevelt, he was said to have run primarily as a means to expose the American public to the party's strong platforms regarding reducing debt and taxes, conserving natural resources, helping farmers, and assuring that both workers and consumers had a fair share of the industry's products and profits.

When Babson passed away in 1967 of natural causes at the age of ninety-one, he was buried between his two wives (Grace and Nona) on the grounds of Babson College. They sit behind a neat brick wall at the heart of the campus he founded.

Babson Boulder Trail.

DIRECTIONS

The Babson Boulder Trail is most easily accessed through the Blackburn Industrial Park, where there is ample parking across the street. Walking toward the radio tower, you will find the path that was at one time called Old Rockport Road, beginning just off the pavement. Head to the left of the tower and follow the trail, where you will be quickly urged to "Get a Job!"

The graves of Roger, Grace, and Nona Babson are located near the upper athletic fields off Bryant Way on the Babson College campus in Wellesley, MA. The site is easily reached by parking in the visitor parking lot and walking along the path toward the upper athletic fields. It is in a small brick-walled enclosure to the left of the path.

Spider Gates Cemetery

LEICESTER, MASSACHUSETTS

SITE HISTORY

Nestled in the woods of the small town of Leicester, Massachusetts, just outside Worcester, sits a small pristine cemetery that serves as a private burial ground for the Worcester Friends Meeting of the Religious Society of Friends (Quakers). Without any large mausoleums, crypts, or statuaries, Friends Cemetery displays modest gray stones arranged in neat and orderly rows. Though many of the interments are members of the Earle and Southwick families and date back to the 1700s, the grounds are kept in such an immaculate state that the cemetery gives the appearance of being much more modern.

The most-distinctive features of the cemetery are the low, black wrought-iron gates featuring a sunburst design that many of the public think is reminiscent of spiders or spiderwebs, which has earned the grounds the nickname "Spider Gates Cemetery."

It is perhaps the gates that have inspired the imaginations of those who have seen them. The cemetery is frequently included in lists of the most-haunted locations in New England. It has been attached to tragedies that include a tree just inside the gates from which a teen reportedly hanged himself in the 1980s, and a young girl's murder in a cave in the area outside the cemetery walls. Despite the fact that there has never been any proof that either has occurred, and no news or police reports to support these claims have been found, the rumors are pervasive on the Internet and continue to be repeated as truth-based urban legends.

Top: The gates of Friends Cemetery, which gave it its nickname "Spider Gate Cemetery." | Bottom: The rock wall at Friends Cemetery.

MASSACHUSETTS

The Quakers have been particularly plagued by reports of occult practices and paranormal activity. Many have claimed that the cemetery contains the Eighth Gate of Hell, that nearby Kettle Brook is in actuality the true River Styx, that runes were found carved into rocks in the woods along the east wall, that strange voices and roads emanate from the woods, and that a small cemetery nearby can be found only once and then never again.

Also a frequently shared and attempted legend is attached to the gravestone of Marmaduke Earle. The legend states that if you walk around his stone ten times at midnight, call aloud "Marmaduke, speak to me!," and rest your head on his stone, you will hear his messages. So many people have attempted the task that the ground surrounding the stone is bare of vegetation, which likely accounts for another rumor that there are areas in the cemetery "where grass refuses to grow."

Between four stone posts, likely where the original meetinghouse stood, there is a large flat stone typically referred to as "the Altar." Though a naturally occurring phenomenon in the region, the reputation of the spot has led some unknown individuals to hold ceremonies and parties in the spot, which has led to church members routinely removing candles, occult emblems, Ouija boards, and empty alcohol bottles from the area. As a result, the cemetery is now heavily patrolled, and the Quakers do not grant permission for evening visits or paranormal investigations.

AUTHOR'S NOTE

I visited the cemetery on a rainy Memorial Day weekend in 2013. While the gates were stunningly beautiful in person, I can't say that the cemetery had any paranormal activity of note. I had the impression that the spirits of several of the Earle and Southwick family members may be lingering to keep tabs on the cemetery, and that definitely led to a strong sense of being watched and "supervised" to some extent. It was clear that I had been given a provisional welcome to visit politely, and at no time was I nervous or fearful while there. At no time did I hear any voices or roars, outside of the plane that flew overhead to a nearby airport, and I found nothing at all scary at the site. It is a beautiful and peaceful spot despite how notorious a reputation it has unfairly gained.

DIRECTIONS

Spider Gates / Friends Cemetery is located in the woods off Mannville Street in Leicester, Massachusetts. A dirt road, which some maps list as Earle Street, is blocked to vehicular traffic with a yellow metal gate. Walk less than a third of a mile down the road through a wooded area and the Kettle Brook until you reach the cemetery. Though the woods are clearly labeled as "No Trespassing" and are part of the Worcester Watershed, the road and cemetery are open to respectful visitors during daylight hours. The cemetery is patrolled by law enforcement, with nighttime visits strictly prohibited, and the church requests that you maintain behavior at all times that reflects how you would want others to treat the final resting place of your friends and family members.

ALSO NEARBY

The "Turtle Boy" statue on City Hall Common at 1 Salem Square is the unofficial mascot of Worcester, Massachusetts. Formally known as the Burnside Fountain, in memoriam of Samuel Burnside, a prominent lawyer in the community, the patinaed statue of a naked boy riding a sea turtle sits on a pink-granite base. While attempting to be playful and whimsical, the statue has often been misinterpreted as an endorsement of bestiality. The detail and expression in the faces are often seen both as charming and disarming. Stolen and returned in 1970, with a thwarted attempt in 2004, many shops in the area now sell Turtle Boy merchandise.

Lizzie Borden

FALL RIVER, MASSACHUSETTS

SITE HISTORY

Lizzie Borden took an axe and gave her
mother forty whacks,

When she saw what she had done,
she gave her father forty-one.

—Children's rope-skipping rhyme

Though there are many inaccuracies in the rhyme all New England
children learned in the schoolyard, it is clear that the legacy of
Lizzie Andrew Borden (1860–1927) lives on. The young woman
was infamous for being tried and acquitted for the 1892 murders
of her father and stepmother in Fall River, Massachusetts. This
"cause celebre" aroused significant widespread controversy and
such heated debate that her innocence or guilt is still highly debated today.

EARLY HISTORY

Andrew Jackson Borden was born in 1822 in Fall River, Massachusetts, and grew into a fiercely determined young man. Though
he struggled financially at first, he eventually found success and
prospered in the manufacturing and selling of furniture and caskets.
He soon became director of several textile mills, including the
Globe Yarn Mill, Troy Cotton, and Woolen Manufacturing Company. He owned considerable commercial properties and became
president of Union Savings Bank and director of Durfee Safe

The murder scene, currently The
Lizzie Borden Bed and Breakfast in
Fall River, Massachusetts.

Deposit and Trust Company. With these positions, he amassed
considerable wealth, estimated to be $300,000 at the time of his
death (equating to $8.3 million in 2017).

He married Sarah Anthony Morse in 1845 and had three
daughters with her: Emma (born in 1851); Alice (1856), who died
at two years old; and Lizzie (1860). Just three years after Lizzie's
birth, Sarah passed away due to uterine congestion and spinal
disease. Emma at twelve years old was said to have vowed on her
mother's deathbed "to always take care of Lizzie" and was instantly thrust into a motherly role that did not diminish when
Andrew took on a new wife, Abby Durfee Gray, three years later.

Despite the family's financial wealth, Andrew insisted they live with extreme frugality. Their home on Second Street was in an affluent area close to his businesses but was not on the more fashionable "Hill" area, where the majority of his contemporaries lived. The home had no indoor plumbing or running water—using a pump room—and no gas lights were allowed, only kerosene lamps.

Additional restrictions were placed on Emma and Lizzie, and they were not permitted to partake in the normal social activities that their peers were granted. Instead of concerts and parties, the Borden girls were only allowed to attend school and events related to their strict religious upbringing at Central Congregational Church. Though Lizzie went to Fall River High School, she wasn't a great student and dropped out her junior year. After a pattern of shoplifting at McWhirr Department Store, Mr. Borden tightened his rein and encouraged more-religious pursuits. Lizzie taught Sunday school for recent immigrants to America and was active in the Christian Endeavor Society, the Women's Christian Temperance Union, and the Ladies Fruit and Flower Mission.

The girls, as a consequence of limited social lives, spent a great deal of time at the Second Street home. This was at times a tense place; Mr. Borden was overbearing, and the girls' relationship with their stepmother was cool. They referred to her as "Mrs. Borden" in the years preceding the crime, and Bridget Sullivan, the family's live-in maid, reported that the girls rarely ate with their parents, and that this coolness was well known in the community.

RISING TENSIONS

Stress and discord in the Borden household spiked in 1892. In May of that year, Andrew came to believe that neighborhood children were coming onto his property to hunt for and look at some pigeons who had settled in the barn behind the home. Andrew killed the pigeons with a hatchet, causing Lizzie, who had just built them a roost, to become greatly upset.

Andrew had also gifted real estate to Abby's sister, and Lizzie and Emma became convinced that Abby was a gold digger out to co-opt Andrew's wealth and their inheritance. They demanded that they be given real estate of their own, and Andrew eventually gave the girls a rental property in which they had lived until their mother's death. They purchased the property for $1 to make it a legal transaction, but sold it back to Andrew a few weeks before the murders for $5,000 (approximately $138,444 in 2017).

In early summer, a broad-daylight break-in occurred at the home, and fifty dollars and some jewelry were stolen from Mrs. Borden's desk on the second floor. Nothing else was touched, and the police were notified. An investigation began, but two weeks later Andrew called it off. Many in the community suspected that Lizzie was up to her filching ways. Though no culprit was ever formally named, from that day on, all doors in the house were kept locked with the key placed in plain site on the fireplace mantle, seemingly to dare the perpetrator to try to repeat the crime.

In July, an unknown family argument caused both sisters to take "extended vacations" to New Bedford, Massachusetts. Lizzie returned to Fall River about a week before the murders but stayed in a rooming house for several days before returning home. Once home, Lizzie and the remainder of the family became violently ill. A family friend later speculated it was from leftover mutton left on the stove and used for several days, but Abby had told a friend that she feared poisoning, since Andrew's shrewd business nature did not make him a popular man.

Finally, an unannounced visit by Sarah's brother, John V. Morse, to the house led to an invitation to stay a few days. However, Morse stayed only one night after a business discussion with Andrew aggravated an already tense situation, and he left to visit relatives across town before the Borden family rose that fateful day.

THE MURDERS

Sometime between 9:00 a.m., when Mr. Borden left for his customary walk around the neighborhood, and 10:30 a.m. on the morning of Thursday, August 4, 1892, Abby set out to clean the guest room that John Morse had stayed in the night before. She was violently attacked with a hatchet-like weapon, and forensics indicate that she was facing her killer when the first blow caused her to turn and fall facedown on the floor beside the bed, causing contusions to her nose and forehead. It was at this point that the killer gave her an additional nineteen directs hits to the back of the head until she was assuredly deceased.

When Andrew returned from his walk at 10:30 a.m., he found the side door locked and his key failed to unlock the front door. When Bridget went to the door she also found it jammed and she swore. She heard what she felt was Lizzie laughing at the top of the stairs. This was later deemed notable because Abby's body would have been visible from the top of the stairs through a gap between the bed and the floor, though Lizzie denied being upstairs when her father returned home.

Lizzie greeted her father in the parlor and told him that Abby had been called away to visit a sick friend. She suggested that Bridget go to a department store sale, but Bridget still didn't feel good and went to take a nap. She claimed to have removed Andrew's books and left him to take a nap of his own, but she gave differing accounts of what happened next.

In one interview she stated that she went to the barn to look for material to make sinkers for an upcoming fishing trip, staying twenty to thirty minutes eating pears. When police investigators searched the barn interior they found no footprints in the dust and questioned whether someone could have stayed there that long with that day's heat.

What was clear is that Bridget testified at trial that she was in her third-floor bedroom when she heard Lizzie calling, "Maggie come quick! Father's dead! Somebody came in and killed him!" Maggie was the name of a former maid and what Emma and Lizzie regularly called Bridget. When Bridget made it downstairs, she found Andrew slumped on a couch in the parlor sitting room—struck ten or eleven times with a hatchet-like weapon. One of his eyeballs had been split right in two, suggesting that he had been sleeping when he was attacked, and his wounds were still bleeding, suggesting a quite recent attack.

A local doctor was sent for, and the call was received at 11:15 a.m. at the police station. A crowd quickly gathered around the house, and some were able to enter the house before the scene was properly contained. Lizzie's answers to the police seemed strange and contradictory, and she immediately drew suspicion. She initially reported hearing a groan or scraping noise or distress call before reentering the house; two hours later, said she heard nothing and entered not realizing anything was wrong.

She recounted her tale of Mrs. Borden visiting a sick relative, and asked them to check on her. She sent Bridget and a neighbor, Mrs. Churchill, to check her room to see if she had returned. They were halfway up the stairs when they became eye level with the floor and saw Mrs. Borden on the floor. The blood on her corpse was dried, indicating there had been one-and-one-half to two hours between the attacks.

Most of the investigating officers disliked Lizzie's attitude and changing stories, but none of them checked her for blood stains, due to the questionable appropriateness regarding her gender. They did do a cursory look around her room, and they were later criticized for a lack of diligence. In the basement they found two hatchets, two axes, and a hatchet head with a broken handle, which became the suspected murder weapon. It had a fresh break in its handle, and it was unlike the others in that it appeared to have been made to look dirty. None of these implements were removed from the property that day.

The police returned two days later on, August 6, to do a more thorough search, confiscating the hatchet head and looking through both Emma's and Lizzie's clothing. That evening an officer accompanied the mayor, who formally informed Lizzie that she was a suspect. On the morning of the seventh, family friend Alice Russell entered the Second Street kitchen and found Lizzie ripping up a dress, that she claimed had been covered in paint before burning it in the stove. It was never determined if she was actually disposing of the dress she was wearing on the day of the murder.

On August 8, an inquest hearing was convened, and Lizzie asked to have her family attorney present but was denied, the court citing a state statute that said it could be convened privately. She had been prescribed large amounts of morphine to calm her nerves, and this could have influenced her testimony or contributed to her seemingly erratic behavior, including refusal to answer some questions and contradicting herself within minutes. For example, initially claiming to have been reading a magazine when Andrew returned home and later claiming to be in the dining room ironing. She was also unable to account for why she had claimed to have removed Andrew's boots for him when they are clearly still on in the crime scene photographs.

She was served with a warrant of arrest and was immediately jailed, though the basis of this warrant was later ruled inadmissible, and a grand jury began hearing evidence on November 7, with a formal indictment being handed down on December 2. Lizzie staunchly pled not guilty, and from her initial arrest and throughout her trial she was held in Taunton, since Fall River had no facilities for women.

THE TRIAL

On the morning of June 5, 1893, in New Bedford, prosecuting attorney Hosea M. Knowlton and future Supreme Court Justice William H. Moody began a ten-day parade of circumstantial evidence that they felt pointed to Lizzie's guilt. The inquest testimony was excluded, as was a report that Lizzie had unsuccessfully attempted to buy prussic acid (ostensibly for cleaning purposes) from a local pharmacist the day before the murders, because the judge felt it was too far removed in time from the crime. Instead, they focused on the motives of money, a growing hatred of Mrs. Borden, and ample opportunity with which to commit the crime. They felt there were no other viable suspects, with Bridget Sullivan having no true motive. It was unlikely to have been a business enemy, because it did not make sense to kill Mrs. Borden and then wait over two hours hidden in the home for Andrew to return. Since there was no robbery, it was unlikely a stranger, and John Morse (Sarah Borden's brother) had an airtight alibi and even remembered the numbers of the trolleys he took to his family's home and back. No, Lizzie was the one and only suspect.

Lizzie entered the court on the arm of her ministers, with the full support of her fellow parishioners and feminist groups who felt she was being unfairly persecuted. Minister Buck escorted her to her seat, where throughout the trial she wore fashionable mourning wear and appeared calm despite the mandatory sentence of death by hanging, if found guilty, hanging over her head. In a dramatic ploy to sway the jury, the police exhumed the bodies, removed their heads, boiled the flesh off their skulls, and brought them into the courtroom. When the skulls were uncovered, Lizzie dramatically swooned, which some claimed was staged. When the courtroom recovered from the scene, Knowlton and Moody tried

Maplecroft, the home Lizzie Borden purchased after her acquittal.

to match the hatchet head into the wounds to prove the hatchet was the murder weapon, and they roughly fit, though not perfectly. The heads were then later reburied at the foot of their graves.

Lizzie never testified, and when earlier contradictory statements from the inquisition questioning were thrown out and the prussic acid she had bought was also deemed inadmissible evidence, the prosecution rested and hoped the circumstantial evidence was enough to convict her.

When defense attorneys Andrew V. Jennings, Melvin O. Adams, and George D. Robinson, future governor of Massachusetts, took over the trial, they presented convincing cause for doubt in one single day. First, the hatchet head had not convincingly been shown to be the murder weapon, and no bloody clothing had been found. Lizzie was seen leaving the barn by two different individuals, and a similar axe murder had occurred nearby shortly before the crime, and strangers had also been reported near the house that day. No one in the home had a spot of blood on them despite what should have been a perpetrator covered in blood without an opportunity to clean up before calling for help. In a final move, Emma took the stand as a star witness and testified that Lizzie and Mrs. Borden were cordial, that paint had been present on the dress, and that it was burned at her suggestion.

With the defense rested, the presiding associate justice Justin Dewey delivered a lengthy summary in favor of the defense. His instructions and charge to the jury prior to deliberation were a virtual direction to acquit. The jury was said to have made their decision in ten minutes but stayed out for ninety minutes so they didn't give the impression of having their minds made up ahead of time. Without the inquest and prussic-acid testimony, there simply wasn't enough evidence to convict beyond a shadow of a doubt, and Lizzie was formally acquitted on June 20, 1893.

Though Lizzie had been declared not guilty, the Fall River community remained unconvinced and imposed their own penalty—ostracization. When she returned to church she found all the pews around her family-owned pew were utterly empty. Slowly her friends began to fade away, and within six months, Emma and Lizzie sold the Second Street house and purchased a more lavish one on "the Hill." They named the house on French Street "Maplecroft," and Lizzie lived there for the remainder of her days, refusing to leave Fall River despite the residents' whispers and stares, which followed her everywhere. Lizzie began using the name Lizbeth A. Borden, and the sisters hired a staff including live-in maids, a housekeeper, and a coachman.

Despite the acquittal, Lizbeth was shunned, and she was back in the public eye in 1897, when she was accused of shoplifting in Providence, Rhode Island. Lizbeth loved the theater, despite actresses at the time being considered to be of the same social standing as prostitutes, and she hosted lavish parties for troops from Boston and New York City at Maplecroft. After a particularly raucous fete held for acclaimed actress Nance O'Neil, Emma moved out. Seeking a quiet existence away from public scrutiny, she moved away to Providence and then Newmarket, New Hampshire, under an assumed name. Though she always professed her sister's innocence, she never saw her again.

On June 1, 1927, Lizbeth became ill following a gallbladder removal and died of pneumonia. Nine days later, Emma died from chronic kidney nephritis in a nursing home. They were buried side by side in the family plot in Oak Grove Cemetery in Fall River. Lizbeth had left $30,000 ($830,648 in 2017 funds) to the Fall River Animal Rescue League and $500 ($13,844 today) for the perpetual care of her father's grave. To her closest friend and a cousin she left $6,000 each ($166,133 today) when the estate was distributed. To Emma, she left nothing. Who killed the Bordens remains a hotly debated subject, and although many feel Lizzie got away with murder, the secret may have passed with her. No other suspect was ever arrested, and the killings remain officially unsolved.

The family plot of Lisbeth Borden, as she preferred to be called later in life.

AUTHOR'S NOTE

Many unsubstantiated theories have been explored through pop culture media, including that Lizzie committed the crimes in a fugue state, that Emma secretly returned from Fairhaven to complete the murders and returned in time to receive the telegram, that John Morse was a conspirator, or that an unconfirmed illegitimate son named William perpetrated the crimes after a failed bid to extort funds from Andrew. The rumor mill has even churned out salacious tales of lesbian relationships between Lizzie and Bridget, which enraged Andrew and Abby, and long-term incestuous abuse by Andrew causing Lizzie to snap and retaliate.

No one has ever been able to prove any of these theories, but that hasn't stopped the case turning Fall River into a notable tourist attraction. Thousands of visitors a year travel to the scene of the crime, which currently operates as a bed and breakfast for the more adventurous visitors among them. The nearby Fall River Historical Society holds many items originally owned by the Bordens in an "Echoes of Lizzie Borden: The Borden Murder Mystery" exhibit, including the original alleged murder weapon and crime scene photos and letters written during her imprisonment. Fall River Historical Society curator Michael Martins and assistant curator Dennis A. Binette, authors of *Parallel Lives: A Social History of Lizzie A. Borden and Her Fall River*, are regarded as leading authorities on the life and trial of Lizzie Borden and are enthusiastic guides to the exhibit.

I had visited the Fall River Historical Society and Oak Grove Cemetery and toured the crime scene previously, but I wanted the full experience. After securing our room on the anniversary of the crime, that year made available through an eBay auction, my friend Cat and I made our way down to Fall River and participated in the annual reenactment of the initial crime scene investigation by the Pear Essential Players. These volunteer actors did a phenomenal job of showing how the events of the day unfolded, while having the improv skills necessary to ad lib while interacting with the public.

After a phenomenal dinner at nearby Tap House Grill, at 159 South Main Street, we returned to the B&B to settle into the John Morse Room, where Abby had been slain. They have taken care to maintain the room as it was on that fateful day, with furniture quite similar to the originals, and it was notable that the energy was charged even after a day full of reenactments and hundreds of visitors touring the property. The environment had a totally different vibe than what it had been on any previous visit to the property. Things just felt "off" for lack of a better term.

We enjoyed a private evening tour for house guests only that included the third-floor maid's quarters and the basement where the alleged murder weapon had been discovered, and the spirits of the house began to make themselves known. During our descent from the third floor to the main floor, another house guest said that she had heard footsteps behind her just before her friend felt an unexplained cold draft of air beside her. Later, just before we were heading down into the basement, I was bringing up the rear behind the guide, the two other guests, and Cat when a broom that had not been disturbed by any of their movements came off a two-inch nail and hit me in the arm. Finally, as we turned in for the night, Cat was hit in the side by some unseen hand as she turned out the light, and we were unable to find reasonable explanations for any of these events.

After a horribly unsuccessful attempt at sleep, hearing near-constant noise in the hallway and in our room itself, and feeling as if we were being watched from every corner of the room, I had to take a sleep aid to get through the night. Though the breakfast served was similar to the last meal the Bordens ate and was utterly delicious, the accommodations were comfortable, and it was so interesting to have full permission to wander the property as we saw fit, I initially was hesitant to return or encourage others to visit. Though I do proudly wear my "I survived the night at the Lizzie Borden Bed & Breakfast" shirt and do encourage visits by day and by night, I feel inclined to recommend an evening stay on any night of the year outside of August 4. It appears that the rumors of hauntings on the property do have some credibility, and while some of the past occupants of Second Street have remained on the property, they may not be appreciative of the reenactments and additional fanfare the anniversary brings. As one of the most haunted locations in the United States, do go; perhaps you will be the party to finally bring together this cold case and can put the spirits to rest once and for all.

DIRECTIONS

Lizzie Borden Bed and Breakfast—230 2nd Street, Fall River, MA; (508) 675-7333 or www.lizzie-borden.com for reservations.

Maplecroft, 306 French Street, Fall River, MA (opening for tours in 2017), was recently purchased by the owners of the Lizzie Borden Bed and Breakfast and will be opened for tours in 2018.

Fall River Historical Society—451 Rock Street, Fall River, MA; (508) 679-1071 or www.lizzieborden.org for hours and exhibit information.

Oak Grove Cemetery—765 Prospect Street, Fall River, MA (enter the cemetery though the ornate stone gate and follow the arrows painted on the roadways to find the Borden monument and plots).

Conclusion

Despite being longtime New Englanders, we enjoyed learning more about the wonderful region that we call home. Though locals, there were so many historic locations, scenic vistas, and urban legends that we had never experienced. We hope we have inspired you to dive deeper into the many dark tourism sites that New England has to offer. Safe journeys!

—Summer and Sandra

Bibliography

BOOKS

Balter, Rose, and Richard Katz. *Nobody's Child*. Boston: Da Capo, 1991.

Bartlett, Charlene B., and Jayne E. Bickford. *Cemetery Inscriptions and Revolutionary, War of 1812 and Civil War Veterans of Bowdoin, Maine*. Berwyn Heights, MD: Heritage Books, 2012.

Blanchard, Fessenden S. *Ghost Towns of New England: Their Ups and Downs*. New York: Dodd, Mead, 1961.

Boyer, Onesimus Alfred. *She Wears a Crown of Thorns*. Whitefish, MT: Literary Licensing, 2013.

Boyer, Paul, and Stephen Nissenbaum. *The Salem Witchcraft Papers: Verbatim Transcripts of the Court Records in Three Volumes*. New York: Da Capo, 1977.

Braun, Eric. *Fatal Faults: The Story of the Challenger Explosion*. North Mankato, MN: Capstone, 2015.

Brittle, Gerard. *The Demonologist: The Extraordinary Career of Ed and Lorraine Warren*. Los Angeles: Graymalkin Media, 2013.

Citro, Joseph A. *Green Mountain Ghosts, Ghouls and Unsolved Mysteries*. New York: Mariner Books, 1994.

Citro, Joseph A., and Diane E. Foulds. *Curious New England: The Unconventional Traveler's Guide to Eccentric Destinations*. Lebanon, NH: University Press of New England, 2003.

Corrigan, Grace George. *A Journal for Christa: Christa McAuliffe, Teacher in Space*. Lincoln: University of Nebraska Press, 2000.

D'Agostino, Thomas. *Abandoned Villages and Ghost Towns of New England*. Atglen, PA: Schiffer, 2008.

Draper, H. Hunt. *Hannibal Hamlin: Lincoln's First Vice President*. Syracuse, NY: Syracuse University Press, 1969.

East, Elyssa. *Dogtown: Death and Enchantment in a New England Ghost Town*. New York: Free Press, 2009.

Faxon, David. *Cold Water Crossing: An Account of the Murders at the Isles of Shoals*. North Charleston, SC: CreateSpace, 2012.

Fleischman, John. *Phineas Gage: A Gruesome but True Story about Brain Science*. Boston: HMH Books for Young Readers, 2004.

Gellerman, Bruce, and Erik Sherman. *Massachusetts Curiosities: Quirky Characters, Roadside Oddities, & Other Offbeat Stuff*. Guilford, CT: Globe Pequot, 2005.

Hall, William J. *The World's Most Haunted House: A True Story of the Bridgeport Poltergeist on Lindley Street*. Wayne, NJ: New Page Books, 2014.

Junger, Sebastian. *The Perfect Storm: A True Story of Men against the Sea*. New York: W. W. Norton, 1997.

Lehman, Eric D. *Becoming Tom Thumb: Charles Stratton, PT Barnum and the Dawn of American Celebrity*. Middletown, CT: Wesleyan University Press, 2013.

Longfellow, Henry Wadsworth. *Tales of a Wayside Inn*. Boston: Ticknor and Fields, 1863.

Macmillan, Malcolm. *An Odd Kind of Fame: Stories of Phineas Gage*. Cambridge, MA: MIT Press, 2002.

Mann, Charles E. *In the Heart of Cape Ann: Story of Dogtown*. Gloucester, MA: Proctor Brothers, 1896.

Mayhan, Joni. *The Soul Collector*. North Charleston, SC: CreateSpace, 2013.

McCain, Diana Ross. *Mysteries and Legends of New England: True Stories of the Unsolved and Unexplained*. Guilford, CT: Morris, 2009.

McDonald, Allan J., and James R. Hanson. *Truth, Lies and O-rings: Inside the Space Shuttle* Challenger *Disaster*. Gainesville: University Press of Florida, 2012.

Merchant, Gloria. *Pirates of Colonial Newport*. Charleston, SC: History Press, 2014.

Morgan, Mark, and Mark Sceurman. *Weird New England*. New York: Sterling, 2005.

Ocker, J. W. *The New England Grimpendium: A Guide to Macabre and Ghastly Sites*. Woodstock, VT: Countryman, 2010.

Oliveri Schulte, Carol. *Ghosts on the Coast of Maine*. Port Clyde, ME: Lone Maple, 1989.

Paradis, Summer, and Cathy McManus. *Gone but Not Forgotten: New England's Ghost Towns, Cemeteries, & Memorials*. Atglen, PA: Schiffer, 2013.

Paradis, Summer, and Cathy McManus, *New England's Scariest Stories & Urban Legends*. Atglen, PA: Schiffer, 2014.

Parker, Gail Underwood. *It Happened in Maine: Remarkable History That Shaped History*. Guilford, CT: Morris, 2013.

Robinson, J. Dennis. *Mystery on the Isles of Shoals: Closing the Case on the Smuttynose Ax Murders of 1873*. New York: Skyhorse, 2014.

Rogak, Lisa. *Stones and Bones of New England: A Guide to Unusual, Historic, and Otherwise Notable Cemeteries*. Guilford, CT: Globe Pequot, 2004.

Schlosser, S. E. *Spooky New England*. Guilford, CT: Globe Pequot, 2004.

Sherman, Eric, and David Fiske. *Madame Sherri*. North Charleston, SC: CreateSpace, 2012.

Smart, Dean J. *Skylights and Screen Doors*. Montclair, NJ: Mont Clair, 2011.

Stanway, Eric. *Haunted Hillsborough County*. Haunted America. Charleston, SC: History Press, 2014.

Stone, Edwin M., Christopher R. Drowne, E. G. Windsor, and Henry W. Parkhurst. *Memorial of the Dead: Being Notices of Monuments in Swan Point Cemetery, Together with the Acts of Incorporation, Rules and Regulations, Catalogue of Proprietors, and List of Officers from the Beginning*. Providence, RI: Providence Press, 1870.

Verde, Thomas A. *Maine Ghosts & Legends: 26 Encounters with the Supernatural*. Camden, ME: Downeast Books, 1989.

Walsh, Liza Gardner. *Haunted Fort: The Spooky Side of Maine's Fort Knox*. Camden, ME: Downeast Books, 2013.

Warren, Ed. *In a Dark Place*. Los Angeles: Graymalkin Media, 2014.

Warren, Ed, and Lorraine Warren, with Robert David Chase. *Ghost Hunters: True Stories From the World's Most Famous Demonologists*. New York: St. Martin's, 1989.

OTHER SOURCES

Bastoni, Mark. "Horror on Smuttynose." *Yankee Magazine*, March 1980.

Coles, Barbara. "Spooky Stuff: Blood Cemetery." *New Hampshire Magazine*, October 2012.

Erekson, Keith A. "The Joseph Smith Memorial Monument and Royalton's 'Mormon Affair': Religion, Community, Memory, and Politics in Progressive Vermont." *Vermont History* 73 (Summer–Fall 2005): 117–151.

"Fatal Explosion in Maine Powder Mills." *New York Times*, February 8, 1901.

Friends of the Eastern Promenade. *Eastern Promenade Map & Guide 2016*. Portland, ME: Friends of the Eastern Promenade.

Friends of Fort Knox. *Friends of Fort Knox 2016 Special Events Schedule*. Prospect, ME: Friends of Fort Knox, 2016.

Friends of Fort Knox. *Fort Knox State Historic Site Guide 2016*. Prospect, ME: Friends of Fort Knox, 2016.

Howard-Fusco, Lisa. "More Than Just a Pretty Place." *American Cemetery & Cremation*, January 2015.

Kaell, Hillary. "Marie-Rose, Stigmatisée de Woonsocket: The Construction of a Franco-American Saint Cult, 1930–1955." *Canadian Catholic Historical: Historical Studies* 73 (2007): 7–26.

Littell, E. *Littell's Living Age*. Vol. 13 (April, May, June). Boston: E. Littell, 1847.

Little Rose Friends. *My Heart Speaks to Thee—the Life of Marie Rose Ferron*. Detroit: Little Rose Friends, 1964.

Longfellow, Henry Wadsworth. "Paul Revere's Ride." *The Atlantic*, January 1861.

Luca, Dustin. "On 325th anniversary, city dedicates Proctor's Ledge memorial to Salem With Trials victims." *Salem News*, 19 July, 2017.

Mayo, Karen. "Two Local Authors Publish Book Detailing Decades of Research: Lisbon Women Write History of Gravestones and Inscriptions." *Sun Journal*, April 29, 1993.

New York Parks, Recreation and Historic Preservation. *Bennington, Vermont: The Sought-After Prize 2016*. Albany: New York Parks, Recreation and Historic Preservation, 2016.

Old York Historical Society. *York Corner School 2016*. York, ME: Old York Historical Society, 2016.

"Powder Mill Explosion in Maine—Congressional Nomination—Crime in Rhode Island—Forgery in Boston." *New York Times*, August 3, 1870.

Presumpscot Regional Land Trust. *Newsletter of Presumpscot Regional Land Trust*, Winter 2009–2010.

Seavey, Aimee. "Swan Point Cemetery." *Yankee Magazine*, September 2014.

Shrewsbury Historical Society. *Gazetteer and Business Directory of Rutland County, Vt., for 1881–82*. Reprint. Shrewsbury, MA: Shrewsbury Historical Society, 2016.

Shrewsbury Historical Society. *John P. Bowman's Laurel Glen and Laurel Glen Cemetery in Cuttingsville, Vermont*. Shrewsbury, MA: Shrewsbury Historical Society, 2016.

Souza, Kenneth J. "Seventy-Five Years Later, Little Rose Devotees Still Pray for Sainthood Cause." *The Anchor*, 13 May, 2011.

State of Vermont, Division for Historic Preservation. *State Historic Site—Bennington Battle Monument 2016*. Montpelier: State of Vermont, Division for Historic Preservation, 2016a.

State of Vermont, Division for Historic Preservation. *Vermont State Historic Sites Guide 2016*. Montpelier: State of Vermont, Division for Historic Preservation, 2016b.

Thomas, Jack. "Victims of the Boston Strangler." *Boston Globe*, July 13, 2013.

Town of Windham, Maine. *Windham Parks and Recreation Department—Parks, Trails and Preserves 2011*. Windham, ME: Town of Windham, 2011.

Various. "The Circus: Celebrating 110 Years of The Greatest Show on Earth." *Newsweek Special Edition*, February 2018.

Vogel, Chris, and S. I. Rosenbaum. "True Tales of Murder and Mayhem." *Boston Magazine*, July 2014.

WEBSITES

www.bangorinfo.com/parks.html (accessed June 2, 2016)

www.barnum-museum.org (accessed September 1, 2016)

www.benningtontriange.com (accessed December 4, 2016)

www.biographi.ca/en/bio/moulton_jeremiah_3E.html (accessed September 12, 2016)

www.boston.com/news/history/2016/10/29/25-years-ago-the-crew-of-the-andrea-gail-were-lost-in-the-perfect-storm (accessed December 12, 2016)

www.boston-discovery-guide.com/granary-burying-ground.html (accessed September 1, 2016)

www.boston.gov/education/historic-burying-grounds-initiative (accessed September 1, 2016)

www.centerchurchonthegreen.org/ (accessed January 4, 2016)

www.ct.gov/deep/cwp/view.asp?a=2716&q=325204&deepNav_GID=1650%20 (accessed September 19, 2016)

www.crowsnestgloucester.com (accessed November 1, 2016)

www.cryptozoologymuseum.com/ (accessed February 12, 2016)

www.danversstateinsaneasylum.com (accessed May 26, 2016)

www.easternpromenade.org/ (accessed June 2, 2016)

www.essexheritage.org/attractions/dogtown-dogtown-common-or-dogtown-village (accessed September 12, 2016)

www.explorenorthadams.com/item/houghton-mansion (accessed September 12, 2016)

www.grovestreetcemetery.org/ (accessed January 4, 2016)

www.hoosactunnel.net (accessed September 1, 2016)

www.indianheadresort.com (accessed August 22, 2016)

www.lds.org/locations/joseph-smith-birthplace-memorial?lang=eng&_r=1#d (accessed August 21, 2016)

www.library.unh.edu/find/archives/collections/betty-and-barney-hill-papers-1961-2006 (accessed September 1, 2016)

www.mthopebgr.com/ (accessed June 2, 2016)

www.murderpedia.org/female.S/s/smart-pamela.htm (accessed May 26a.org/female.T/t/toppan-jane.htm (accessed May 26, 2016)

www.newenglandhistoricalsociety.com/the-day-rhode-island-hanged-24-pirates/ (accessed May 2, 2016)

www.paulreverehouse.org (accessed November 22, 2011)

www.piratemuseum.com/edbiogra.htm (accessed May 2, 2016)

www.salem.com/proctors-ledge-memorial-project (accessed February 18, 2018)

www.salemstate.edu/~ebaker/Gallows_Hill (accessed February 18, 2018)

www.spiritsalive.org/index.htm (accessed June 2, 2016)

www.stonehengeusa.com/ (accessed July 14, 2016)

www.swanpointcemetery.com/index.php (accessed June 2, 2016)

www.thedacrons.com/eric/dogtown/visiting_dogtown_gloucester.php (accessed June 2, 2016)

www.wayside.org (accessed May 20, 2013)

www.whereangelsplayfoundation.org/ (accessed May 21, 2016)

www.whitehouse.gov/1600/presidents/calvincoolidge (accessed August 19, 2016)

www.whydah.com (accessed May 2, 2016)

www.wilsoncastle.com (accessed September 1, 2016)

www.1812privateers.org/NAVAL/boxerINDEX.html (accessed June 2, 2016)

PERSONAL INTERVIEWS

Davine, Denise. Personal interview. August 1, 2016.

Kemp, Jeffrey. Personal interview. September 12, 2016.